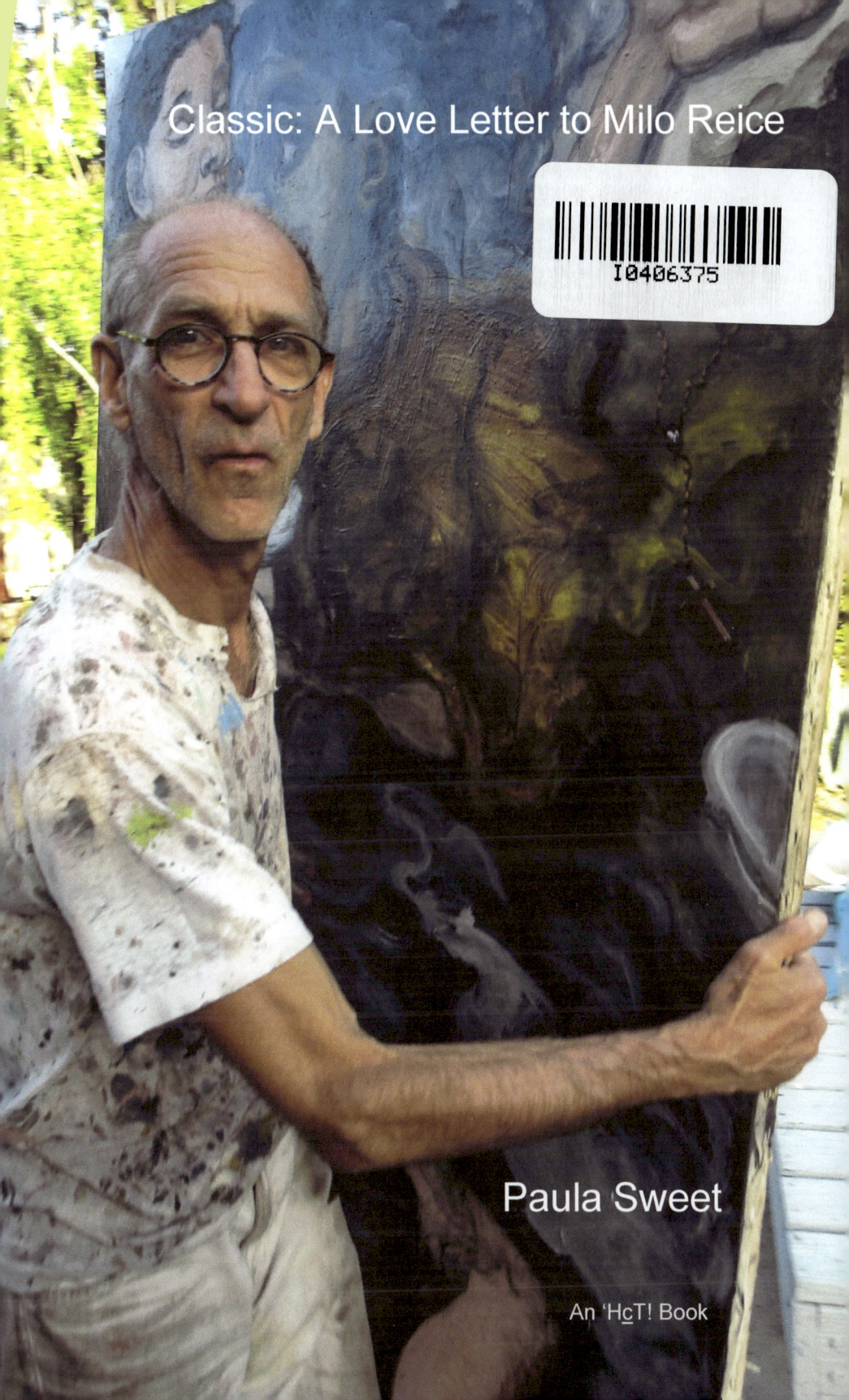

# Classic: A Love Letter to Milo Reice

**Paula Sweet**

An 'HcT! Book

**Classic: A Love Letter to Milo Reice**

Photography ©2016 by Paula Sweet
ISBN 978-1533159519

First edition May 2016

Designed by SMoss

An 'HcT! Book

This book is affectionately dedicated to Carol Chenowith

infinitely more than the good wife

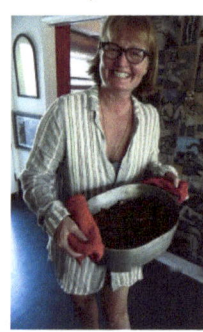 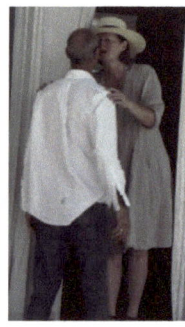

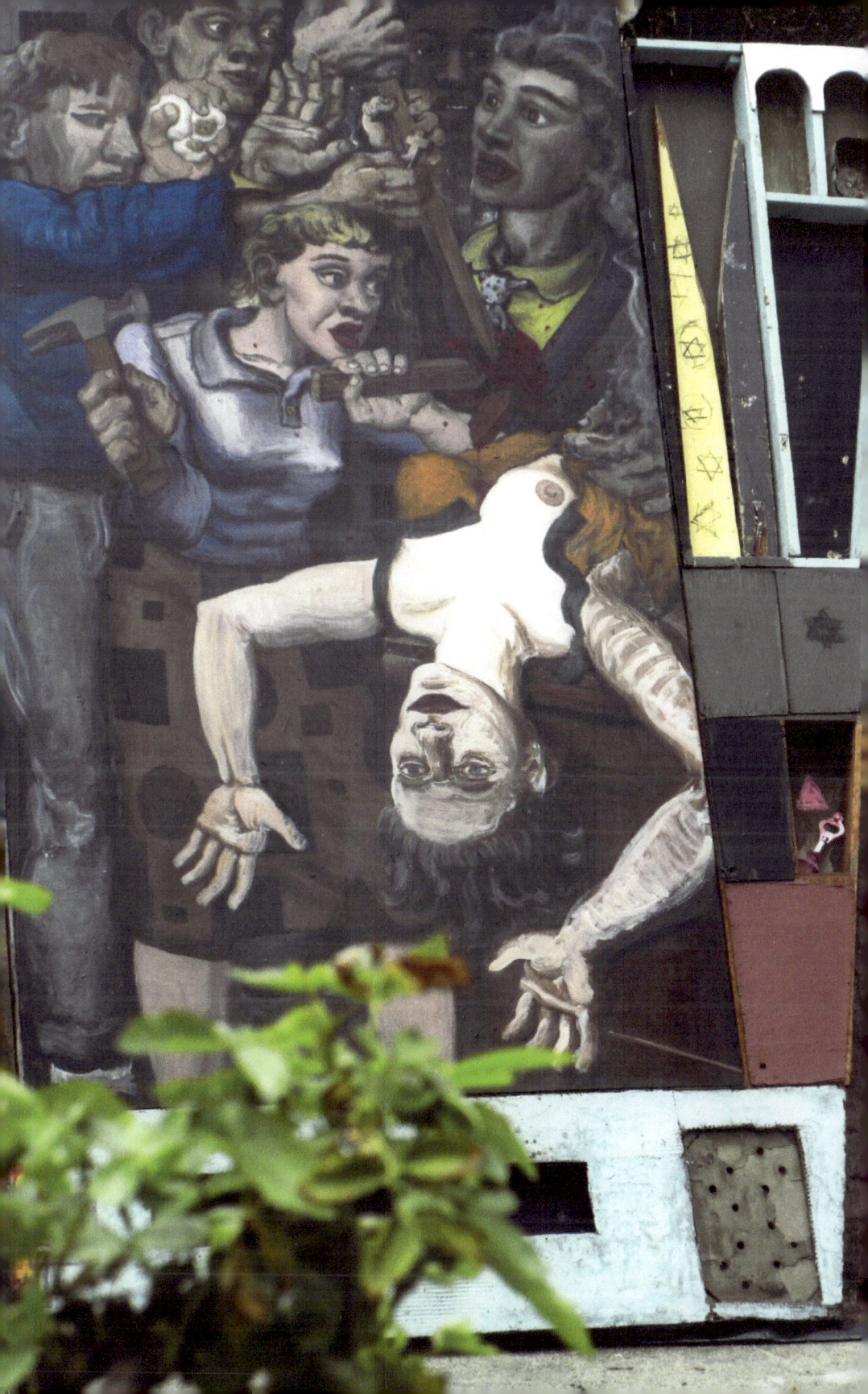

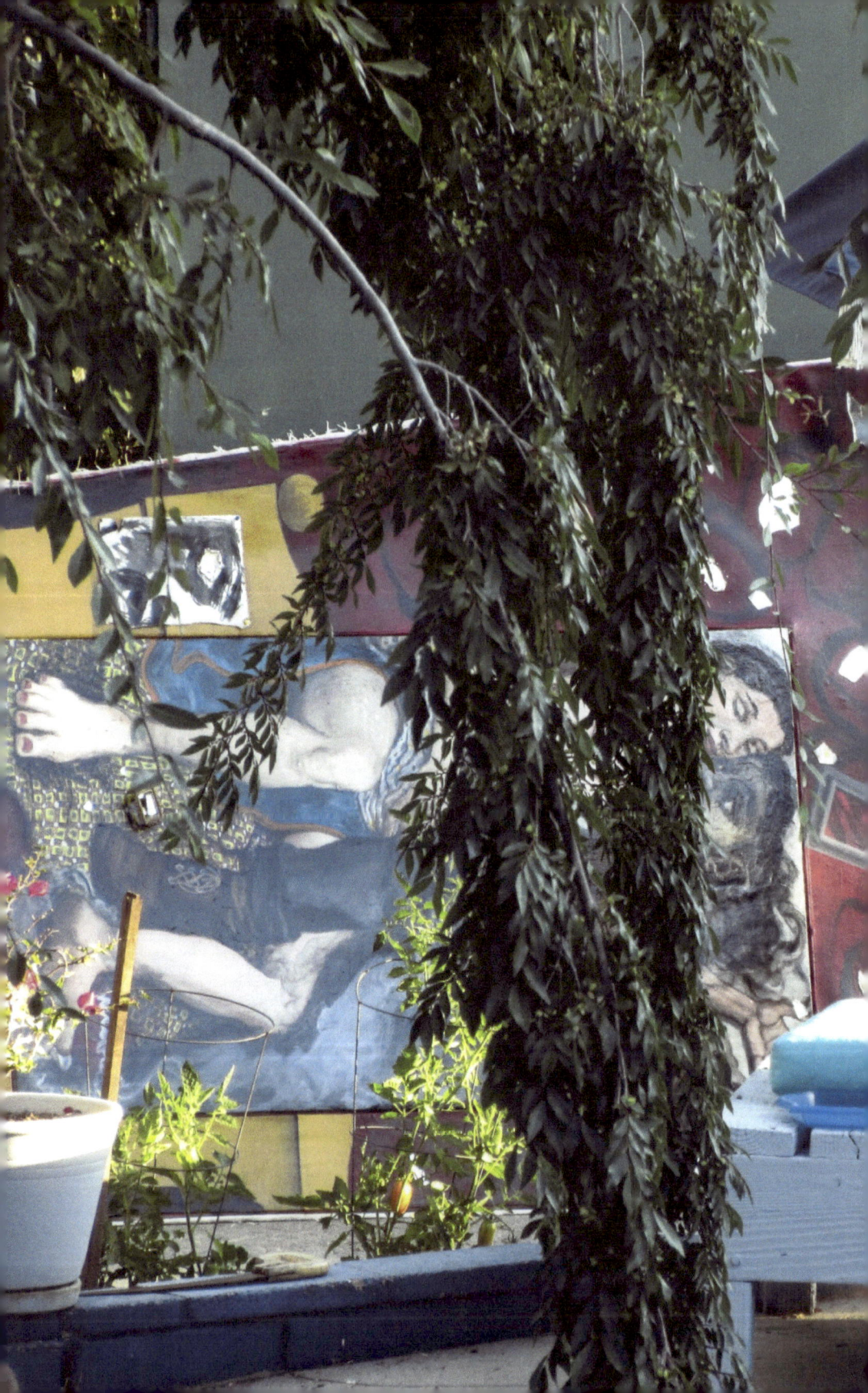

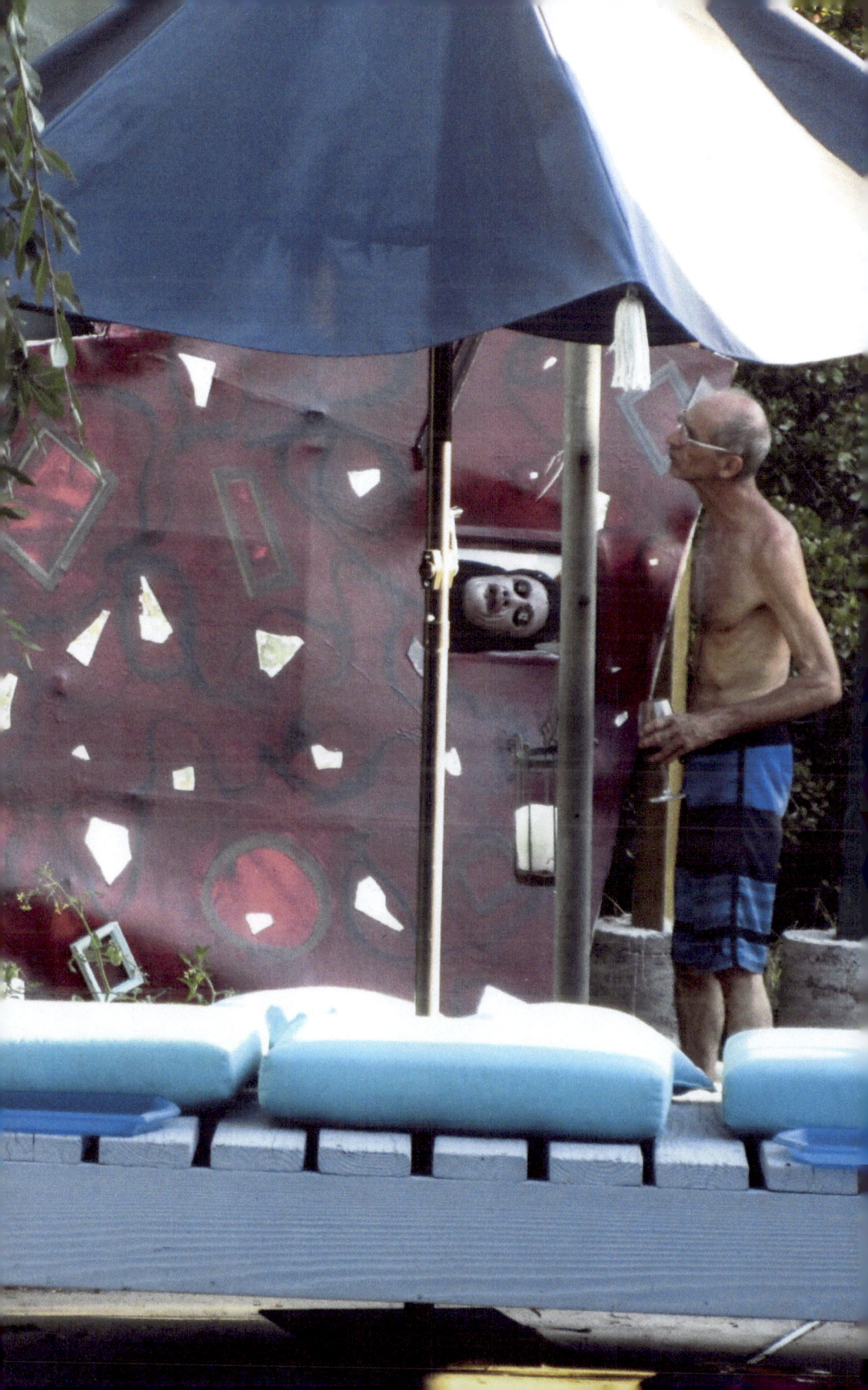

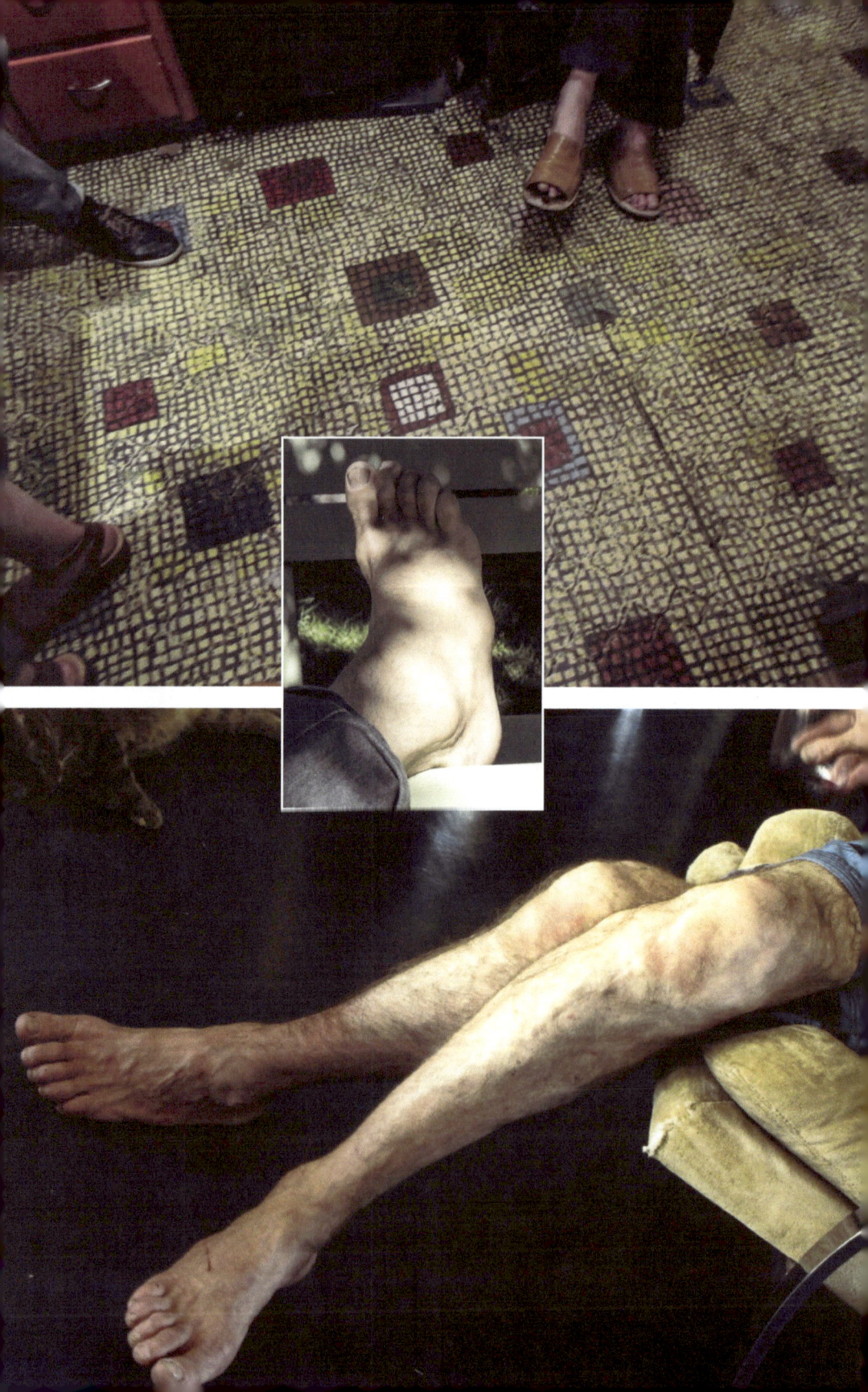

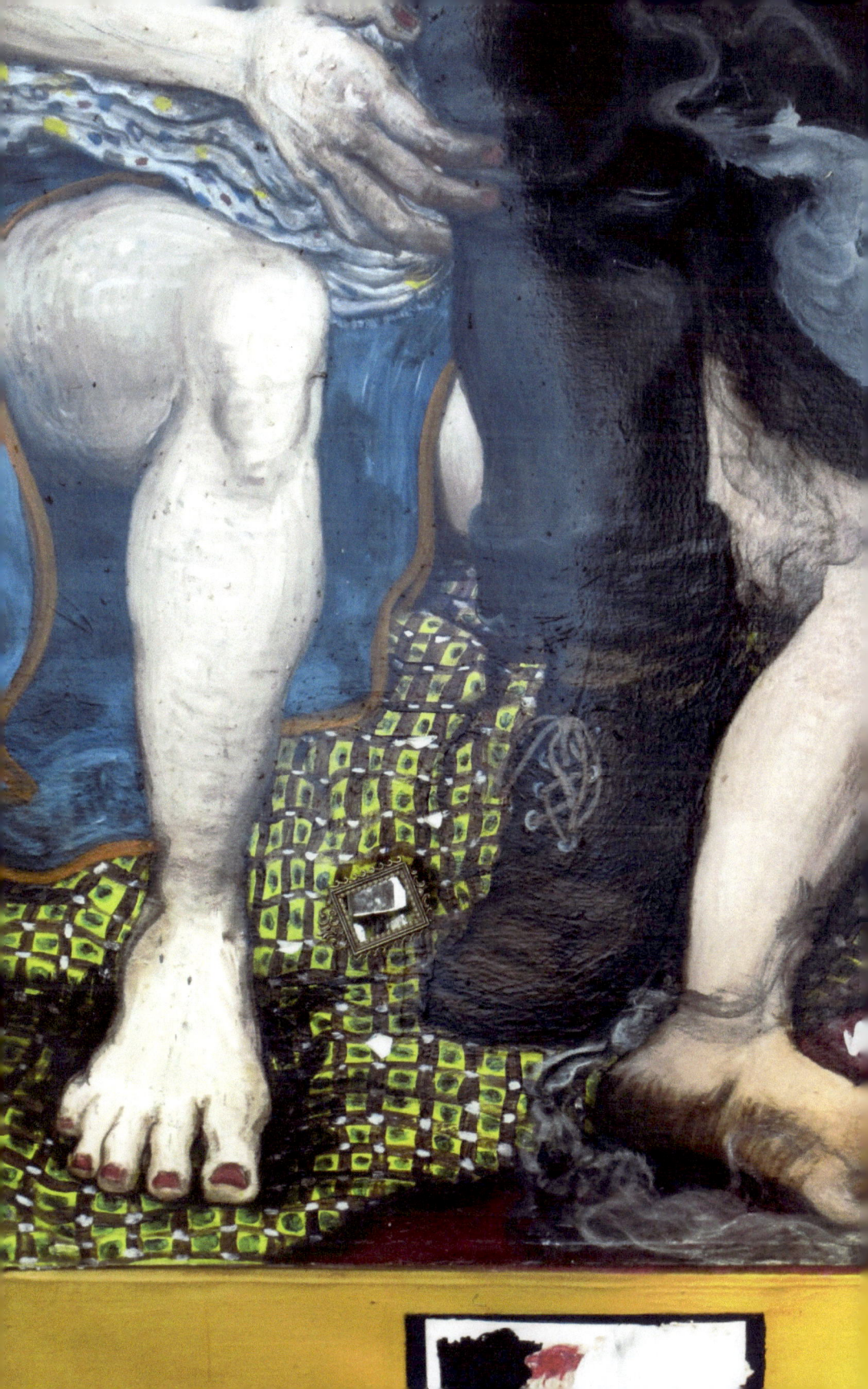

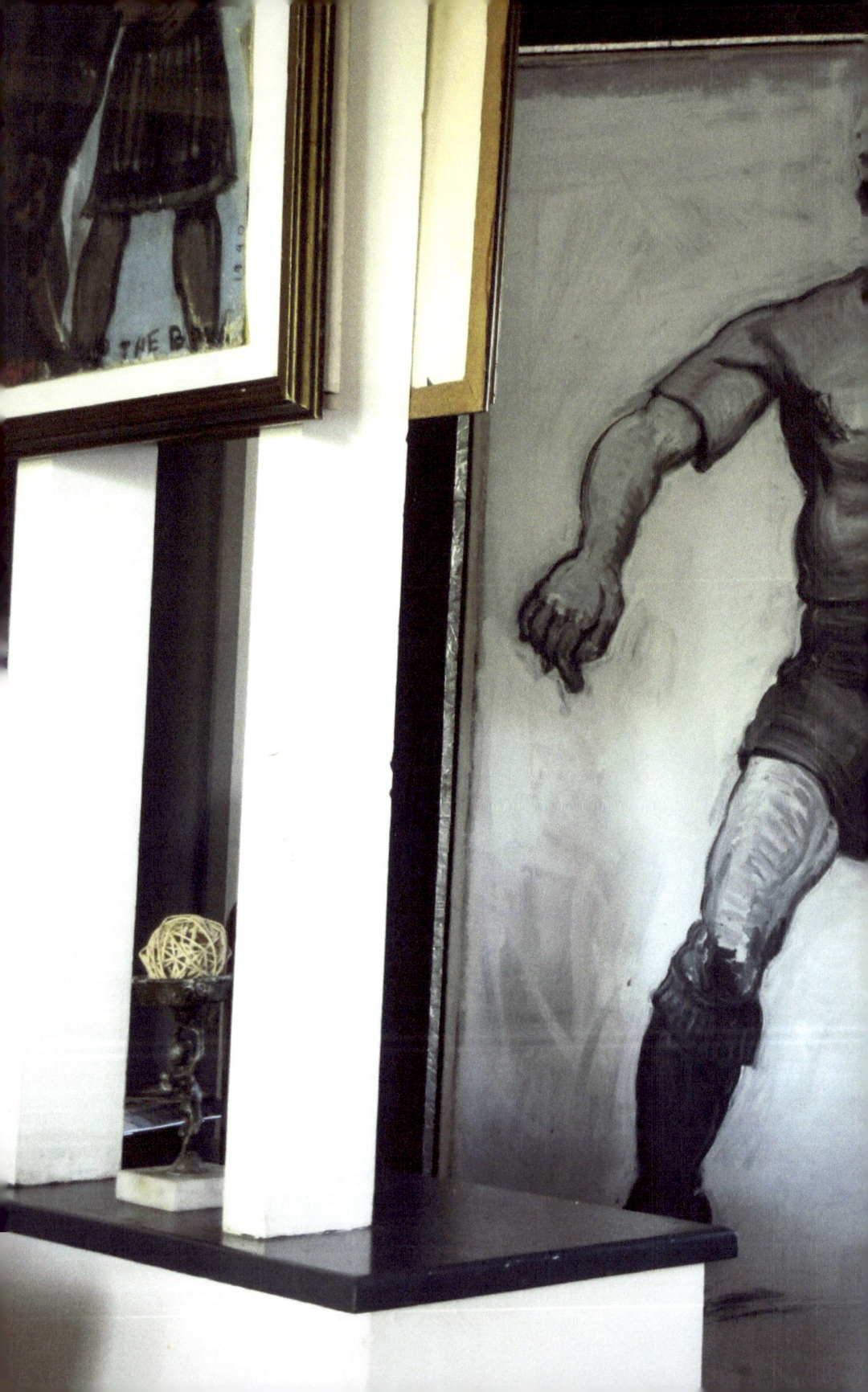

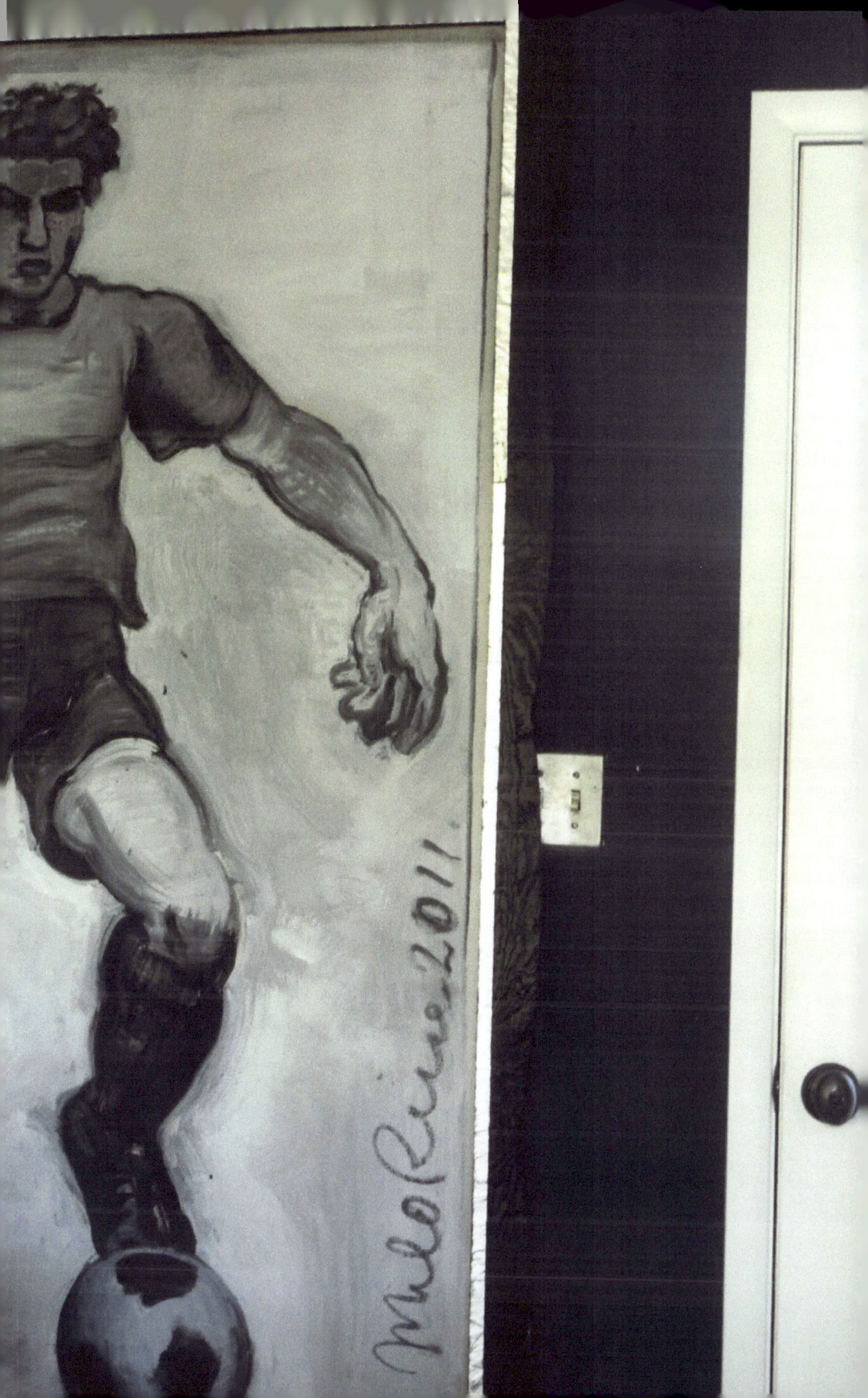

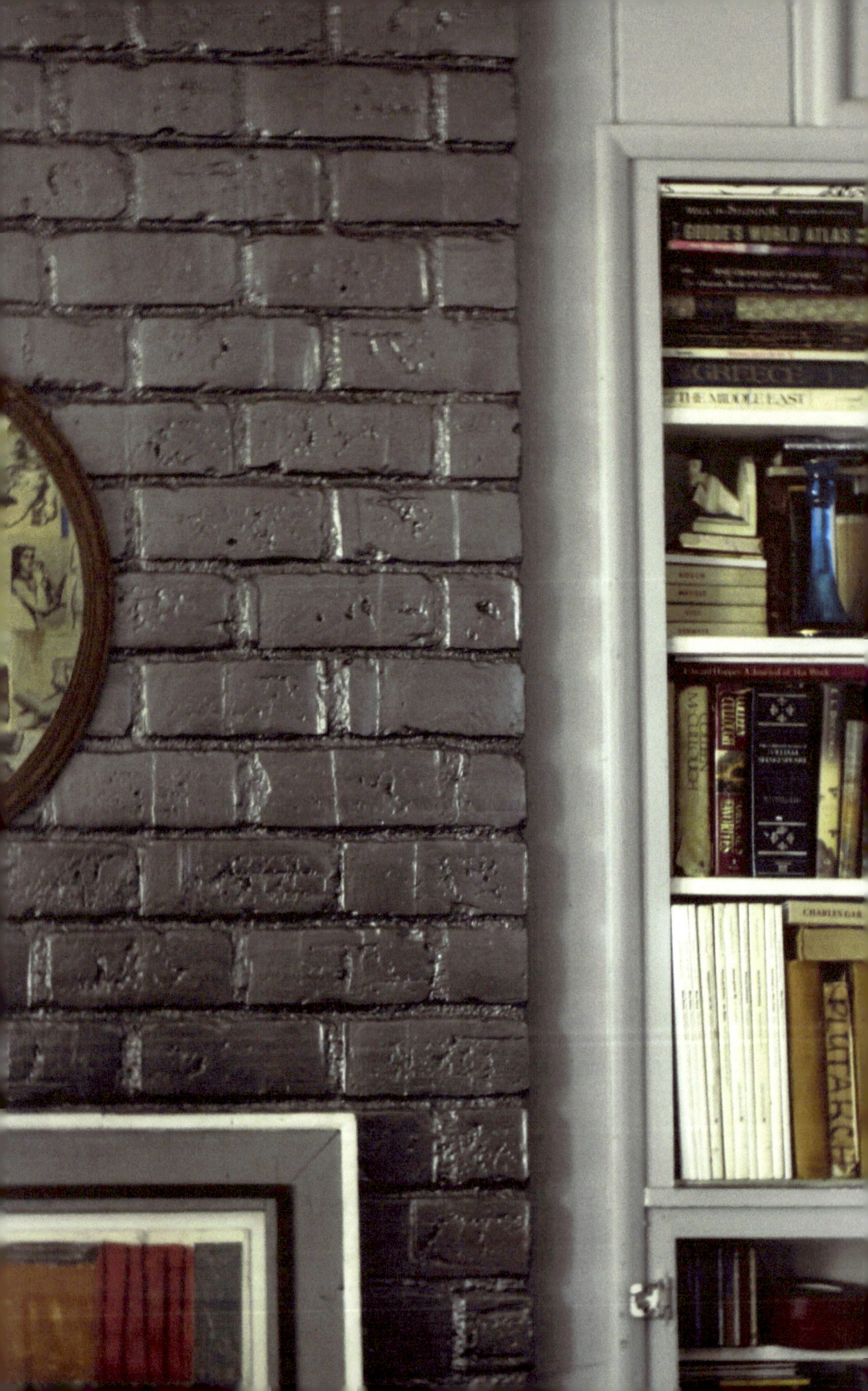

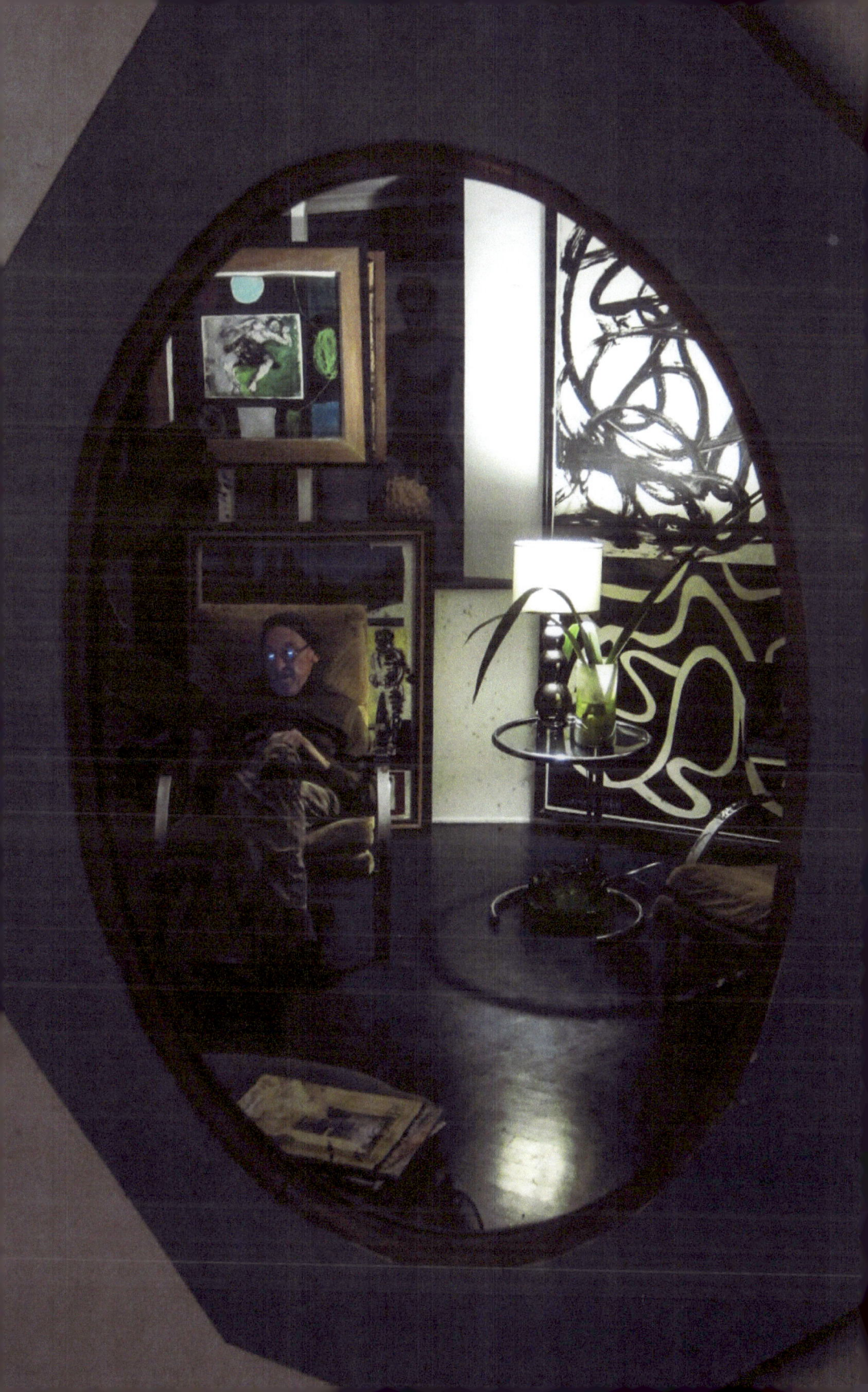

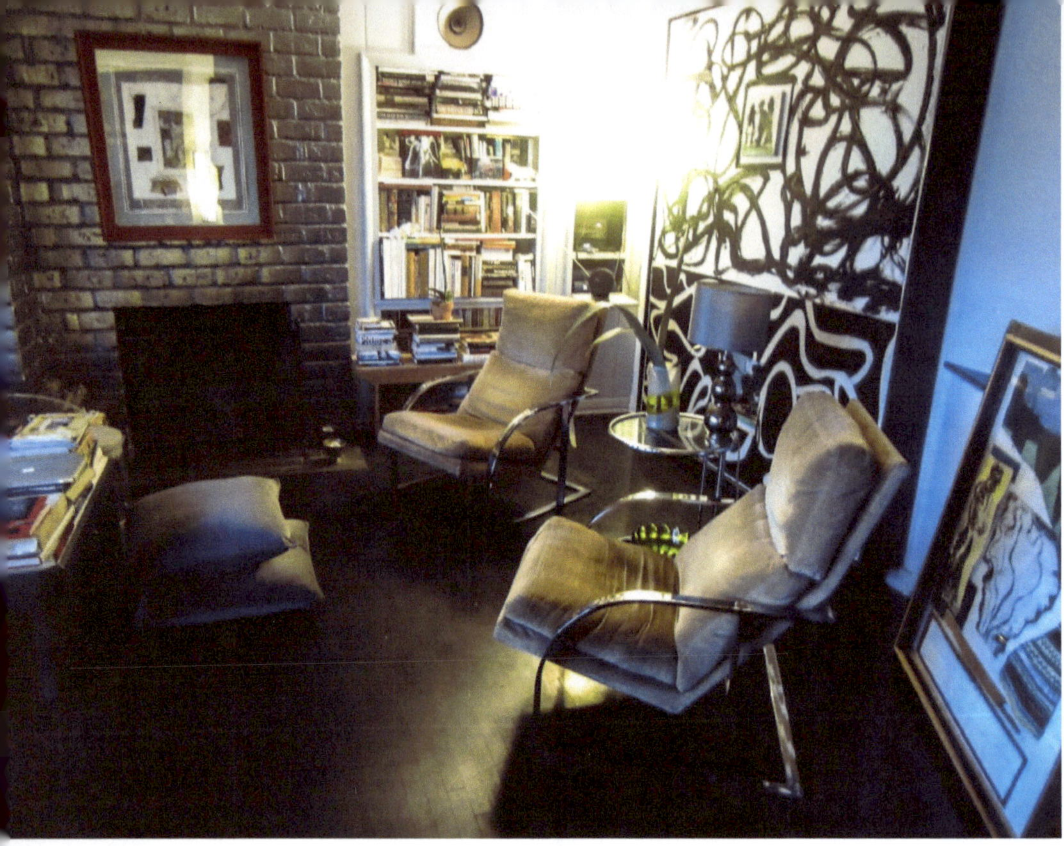

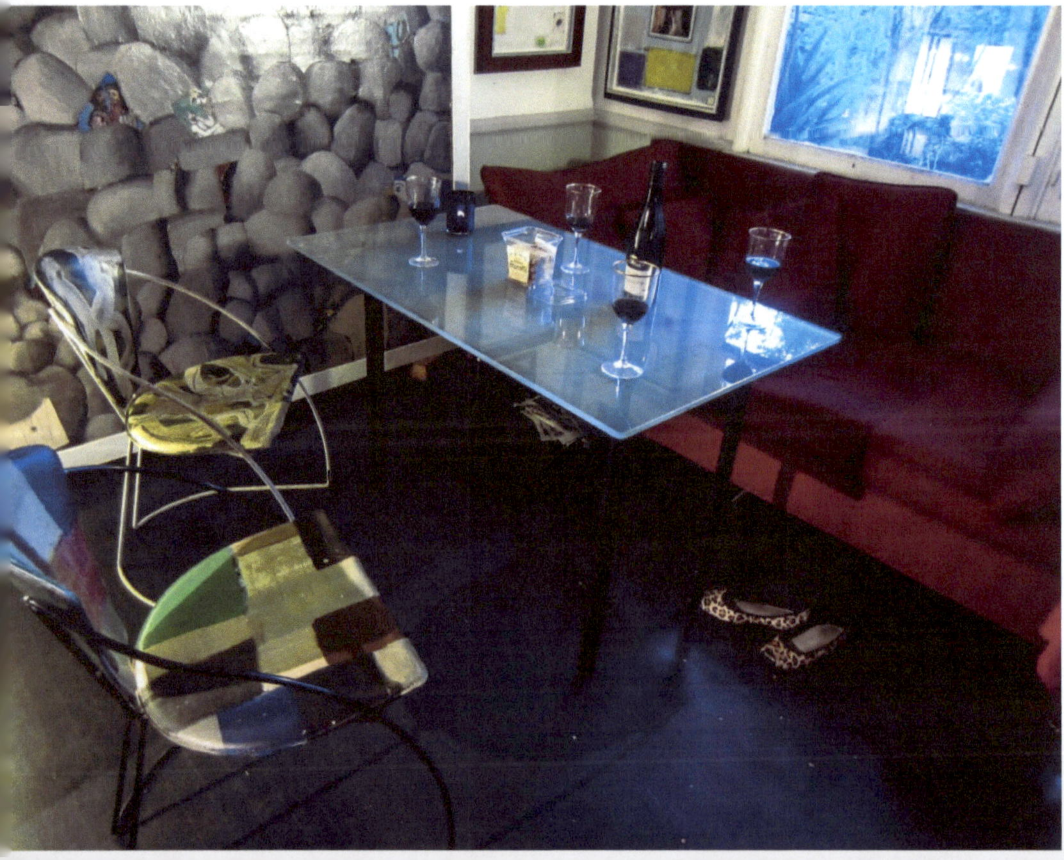

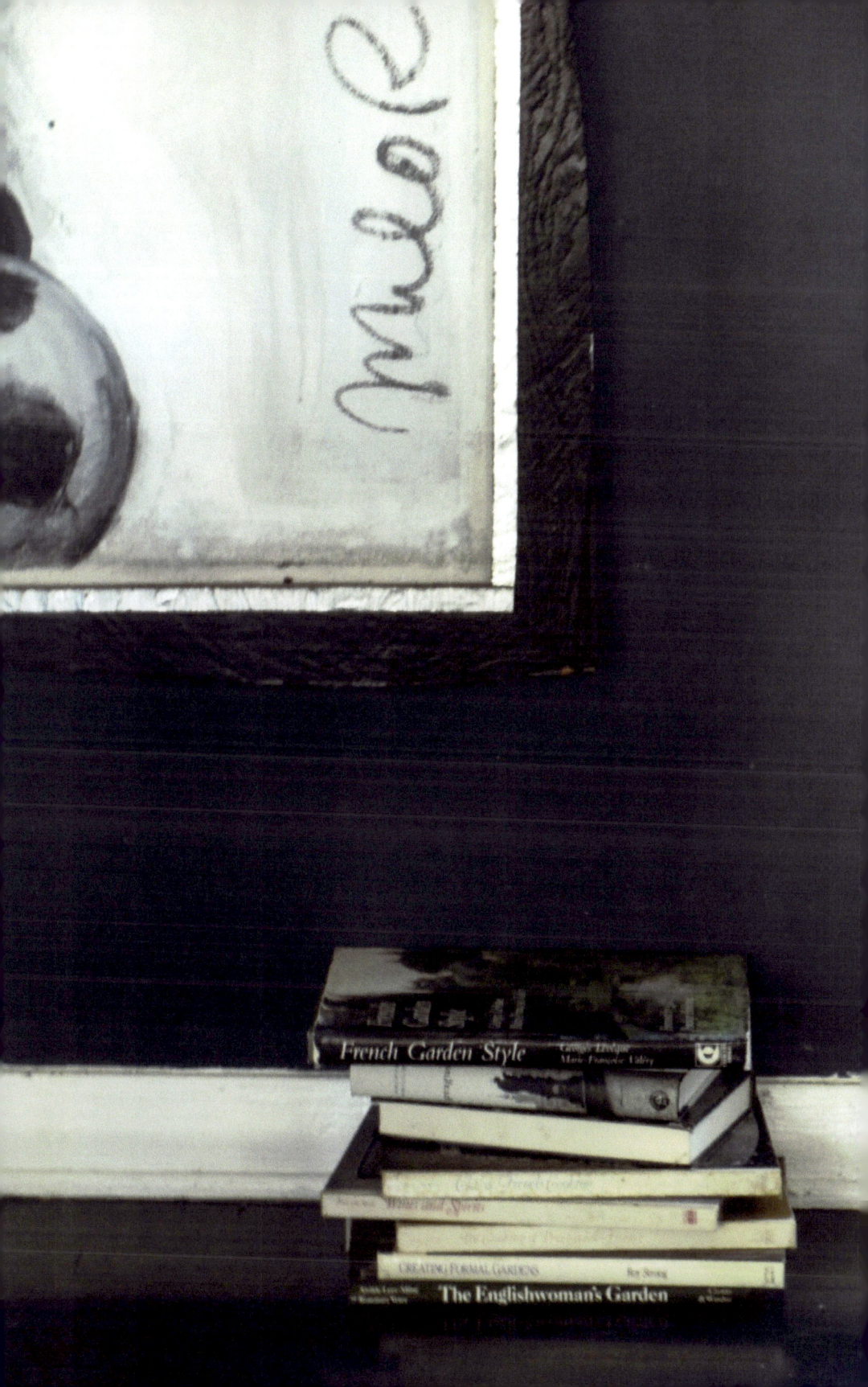

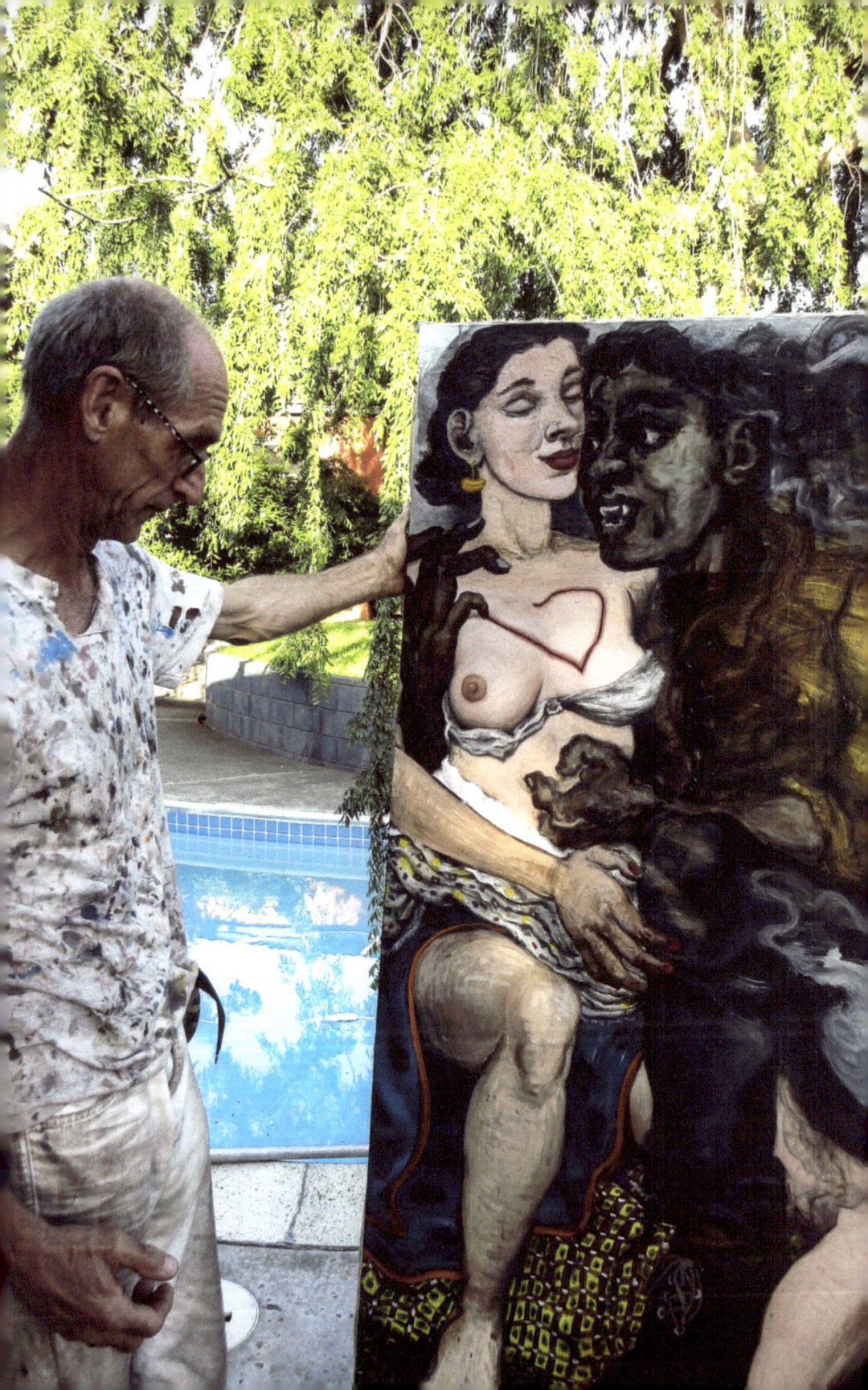

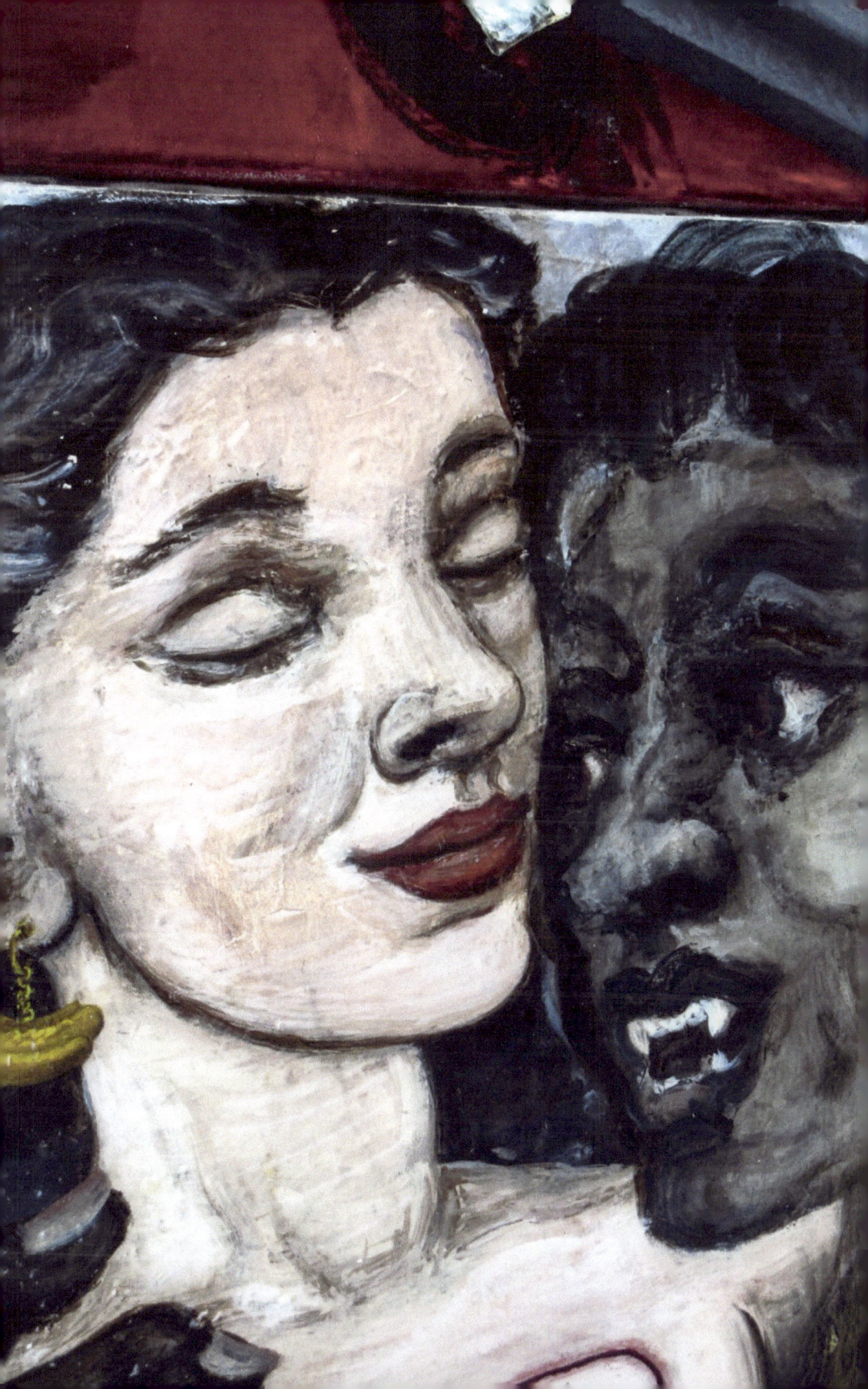

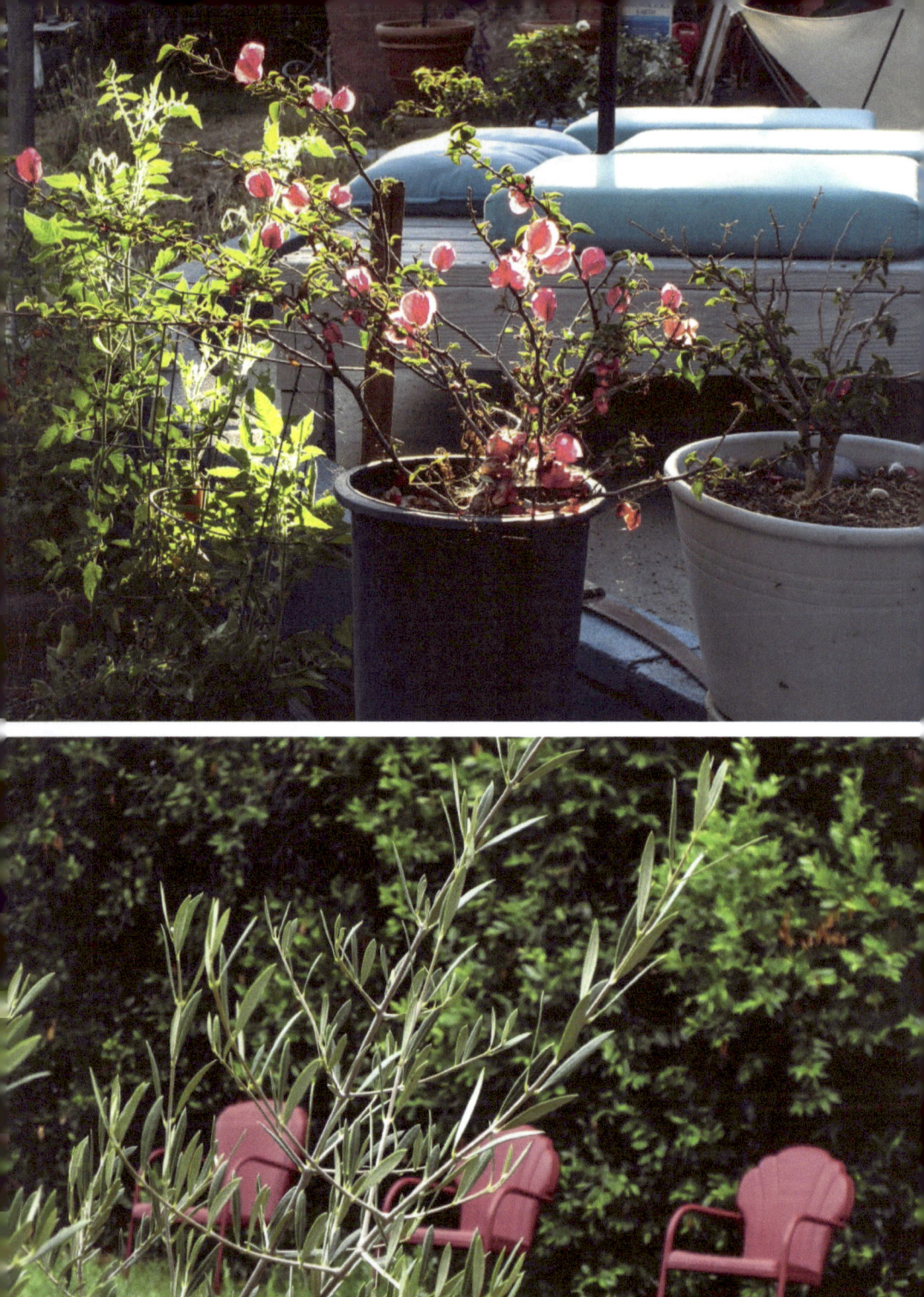

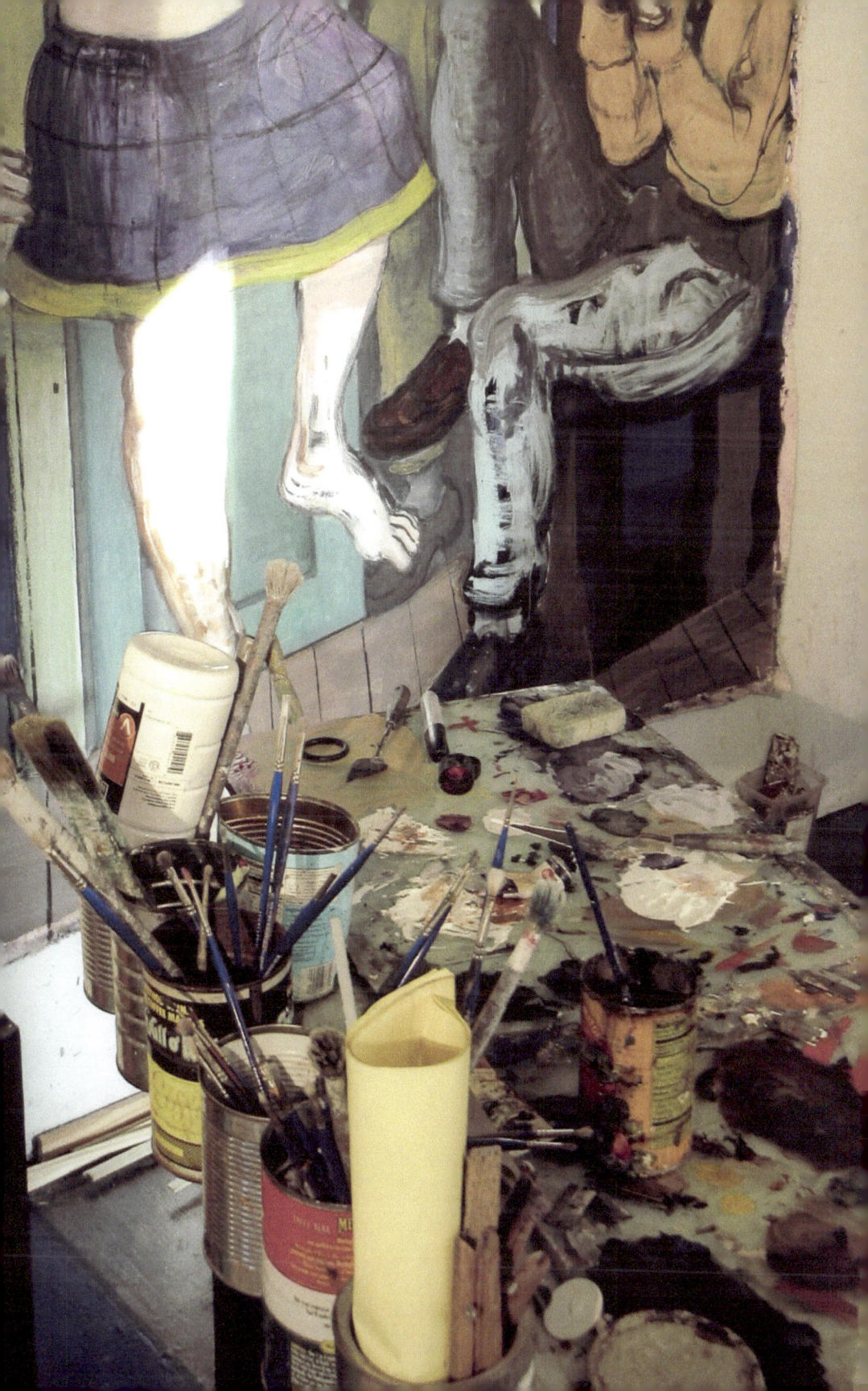

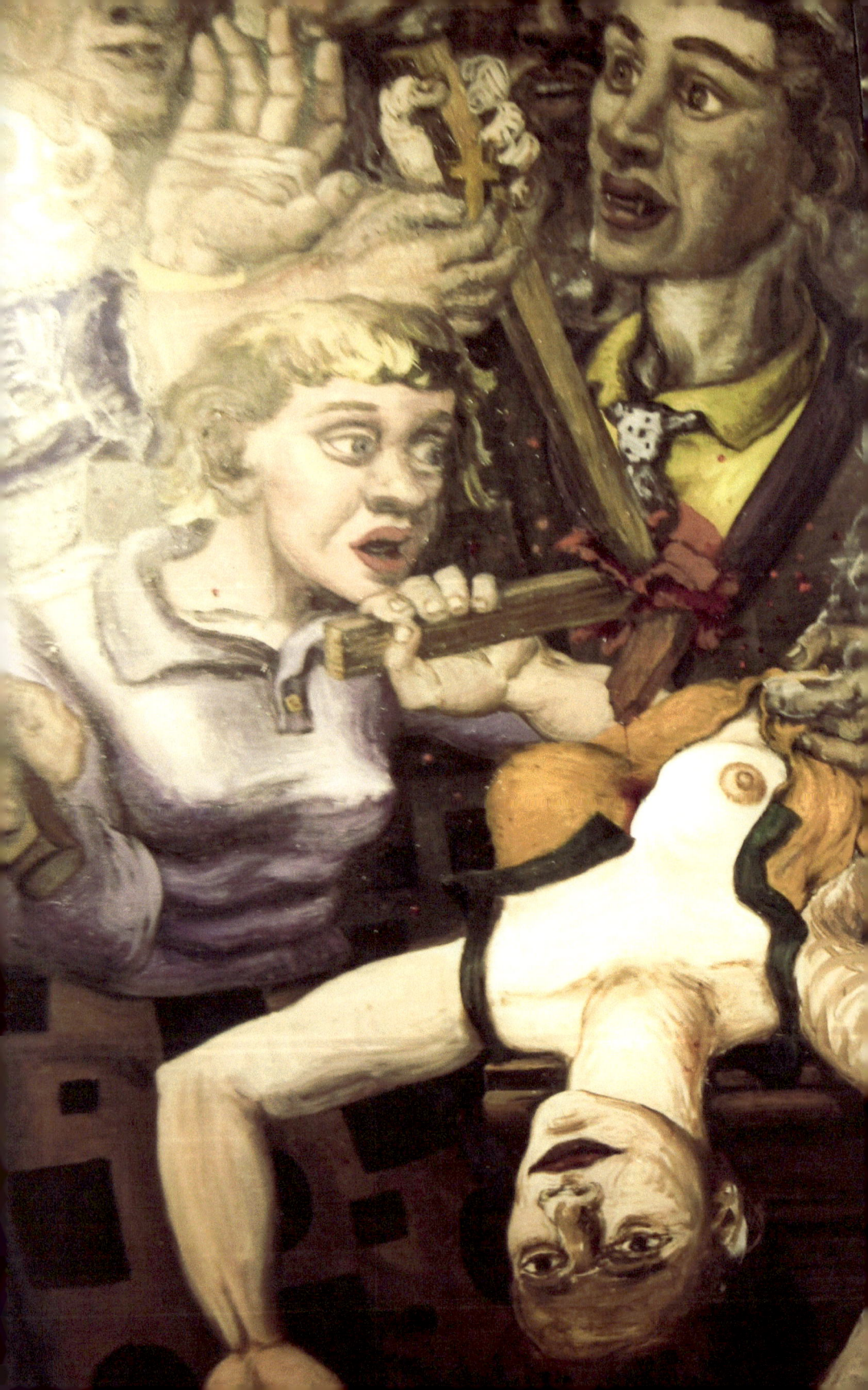

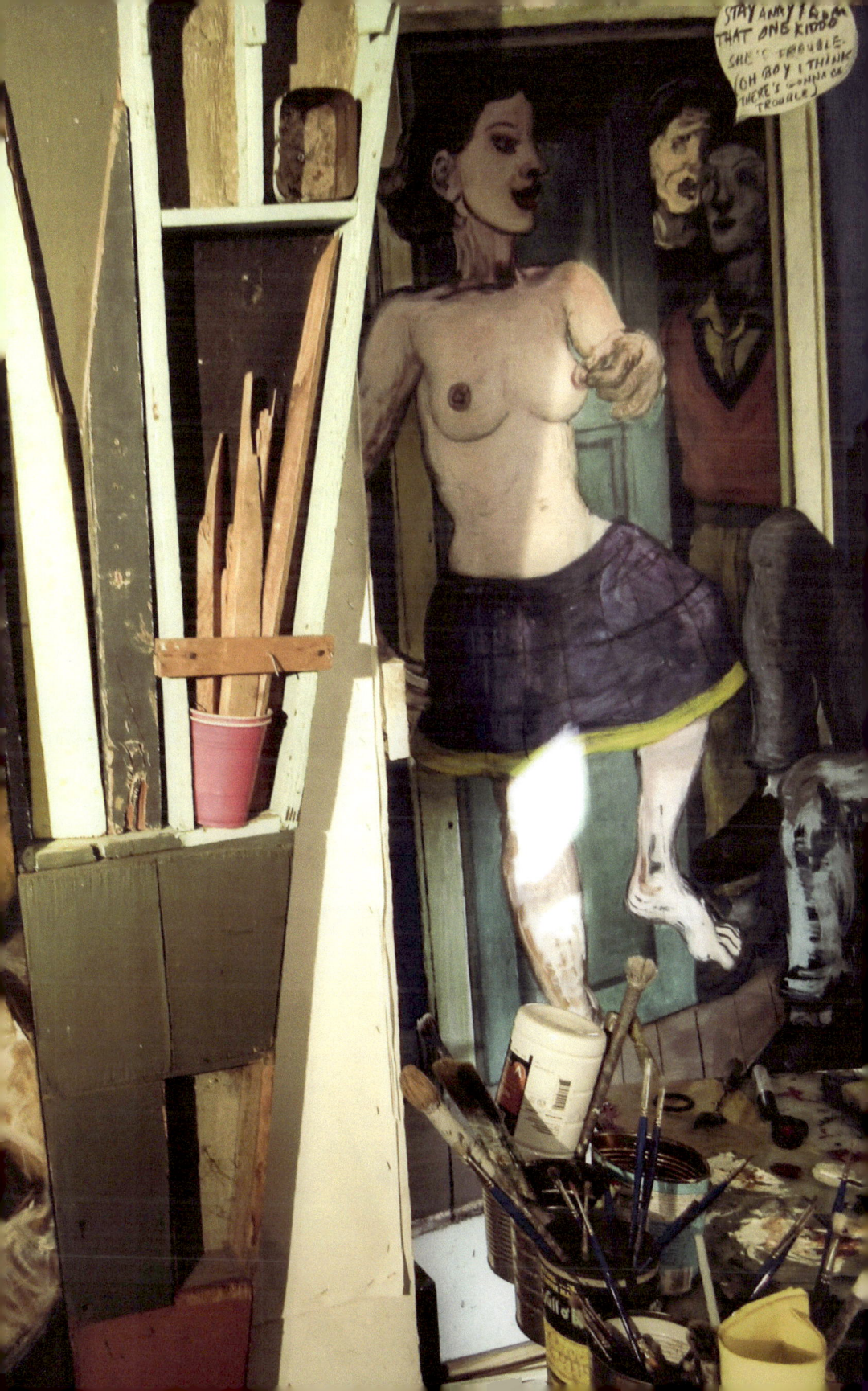

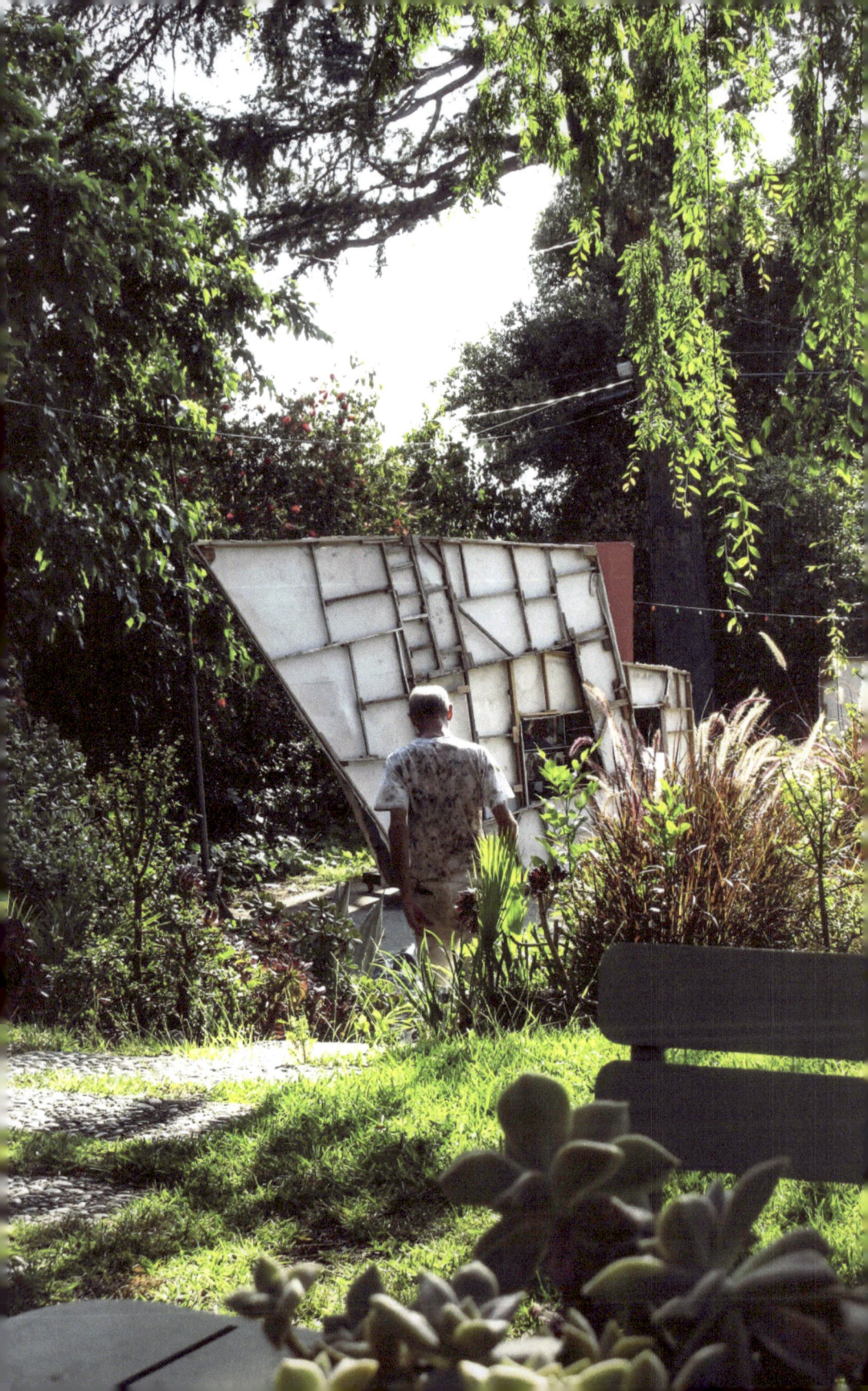

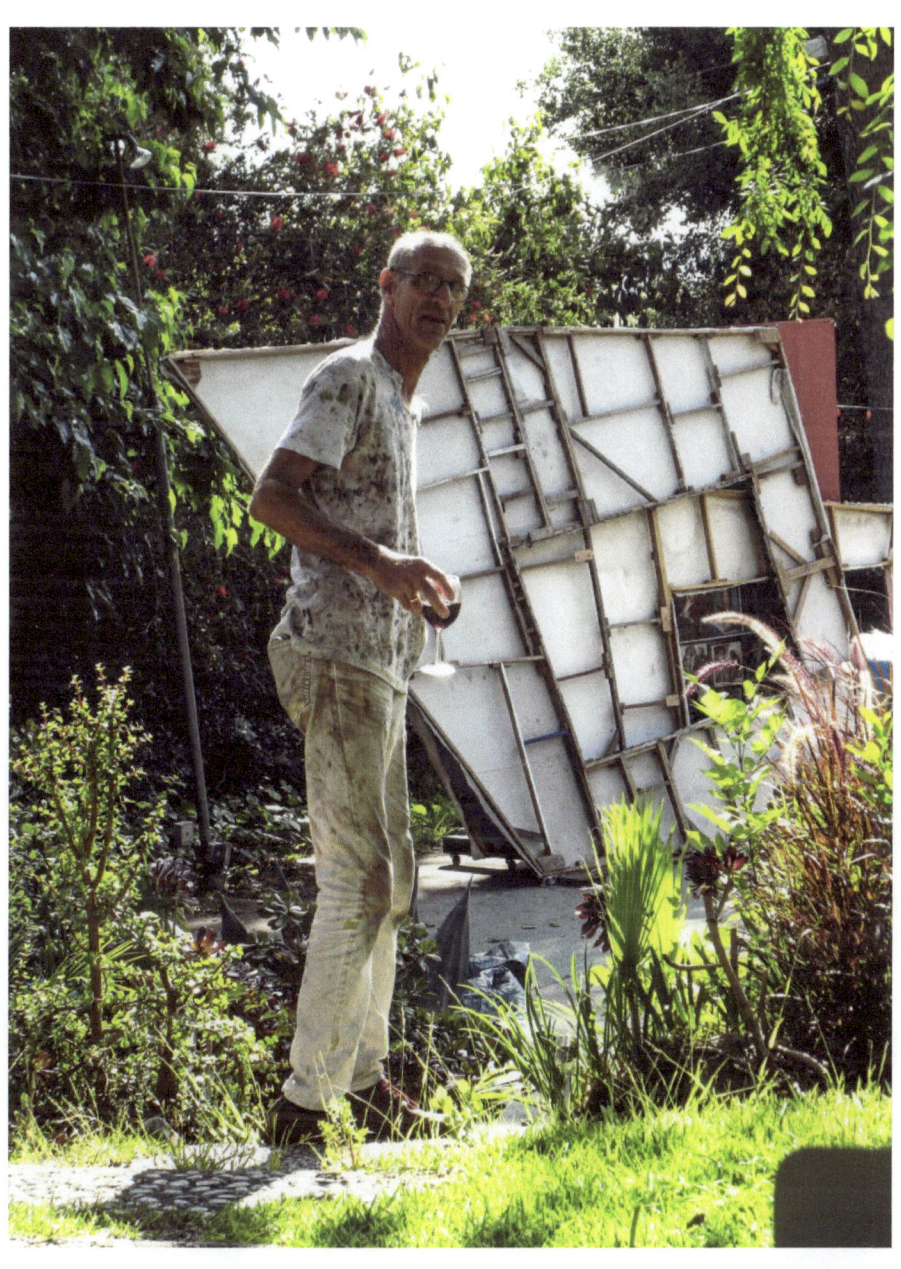

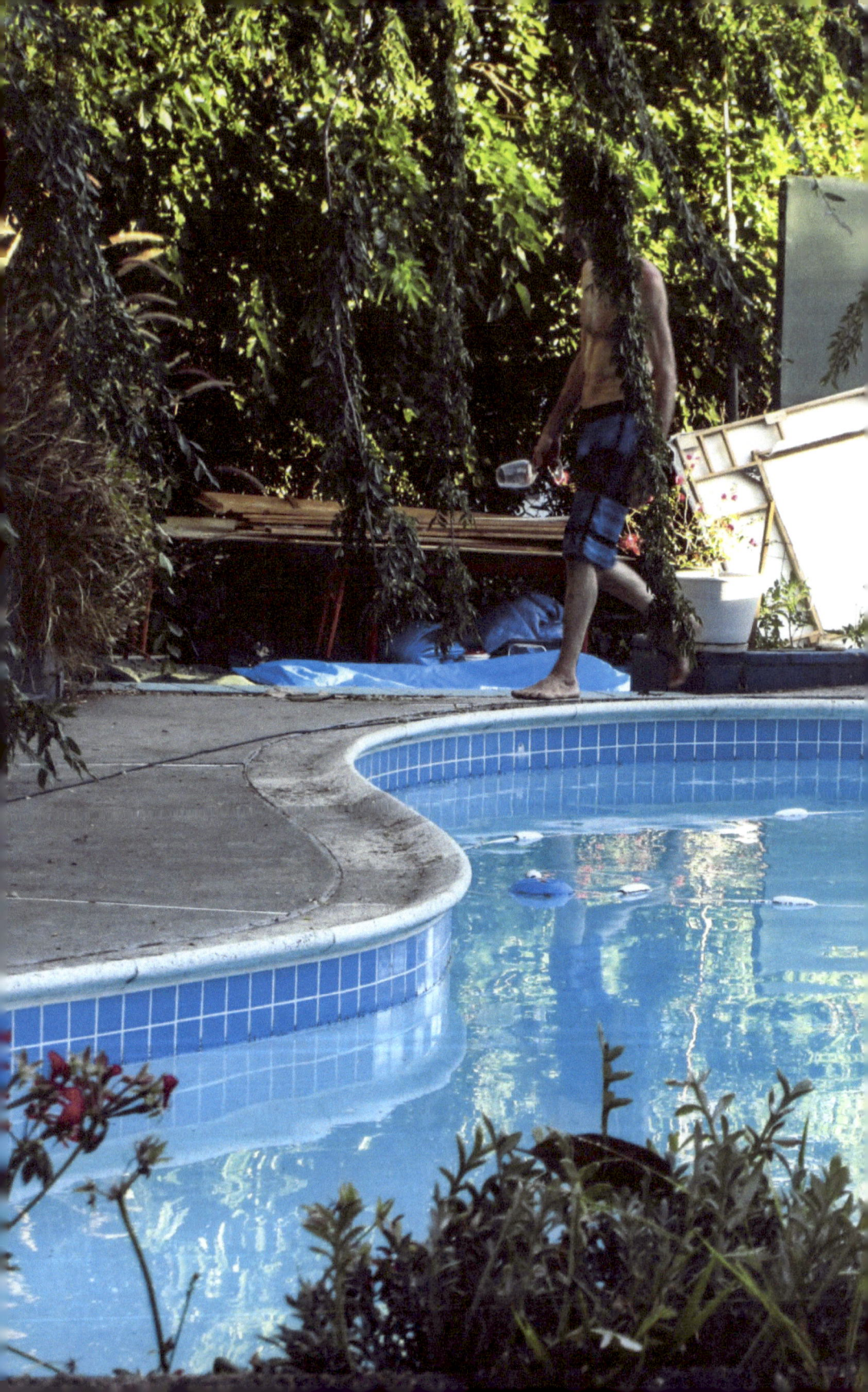

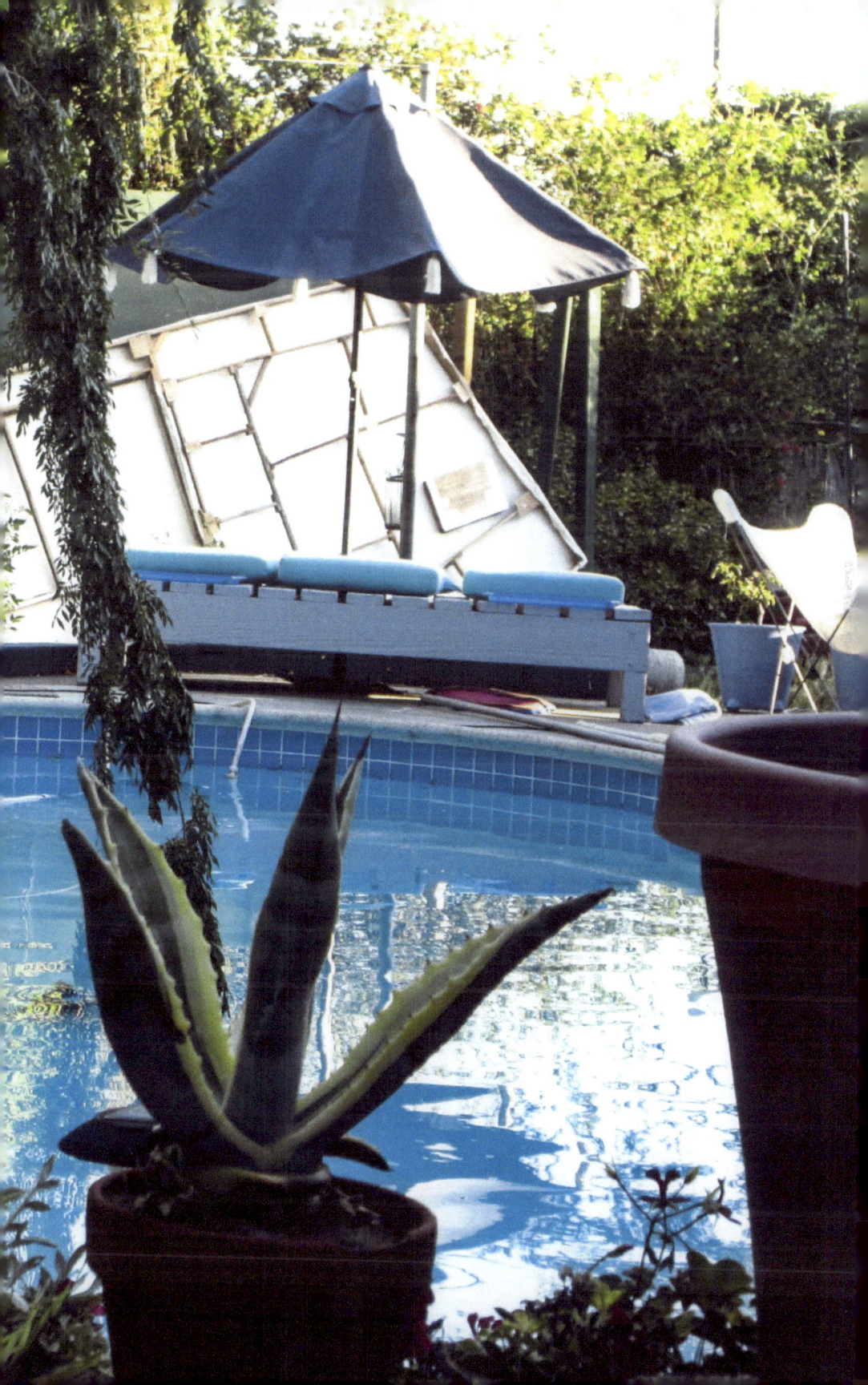

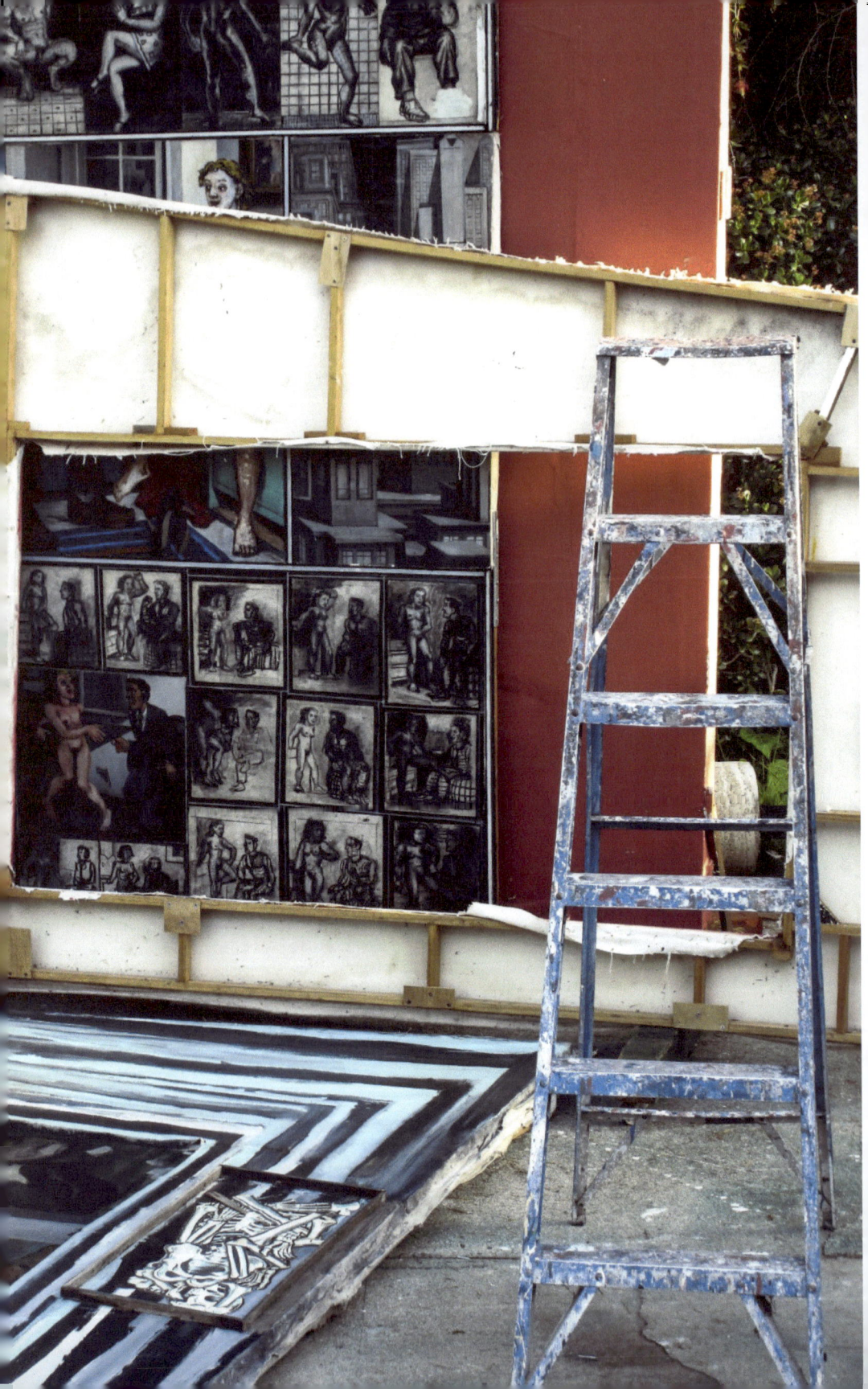

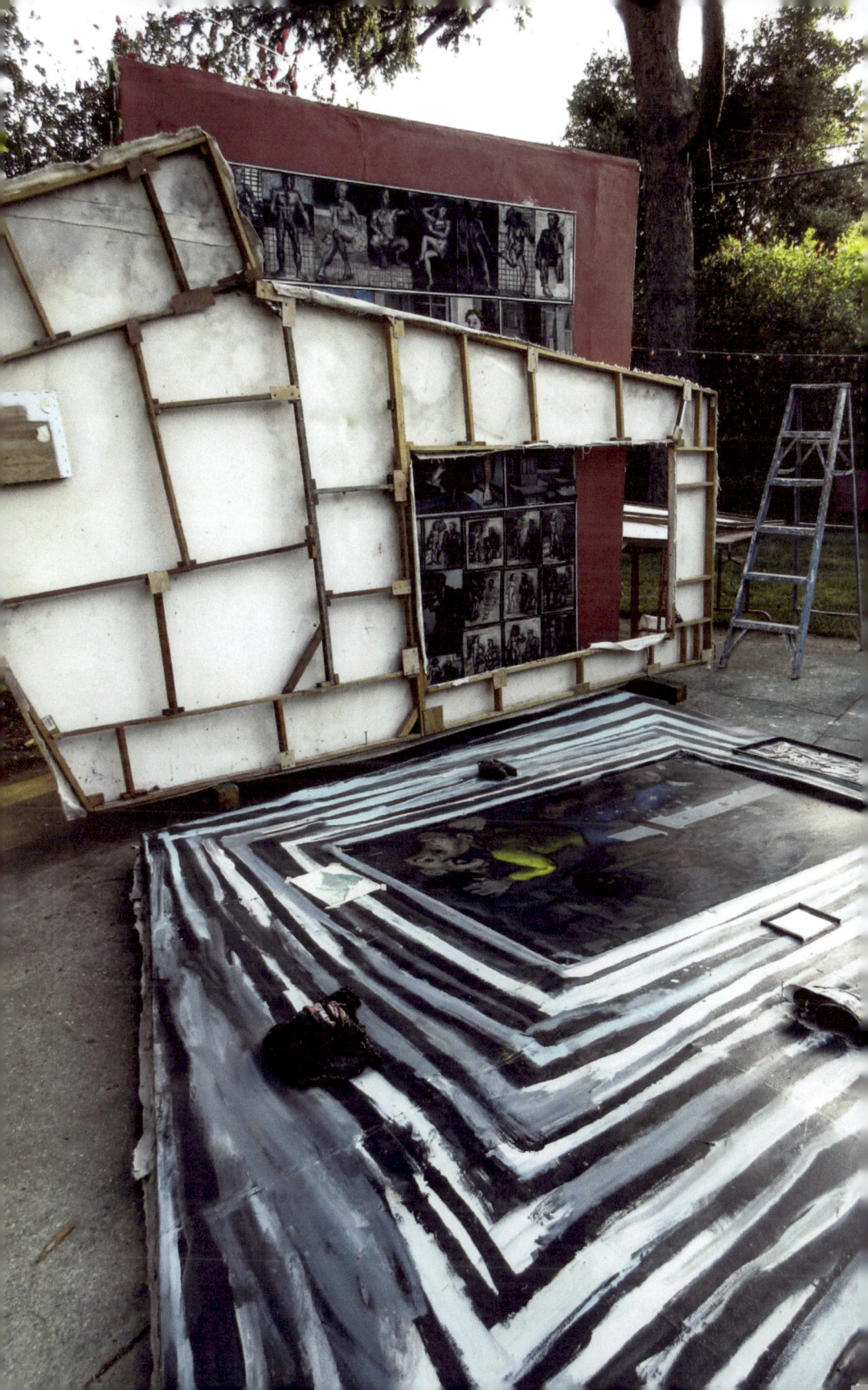

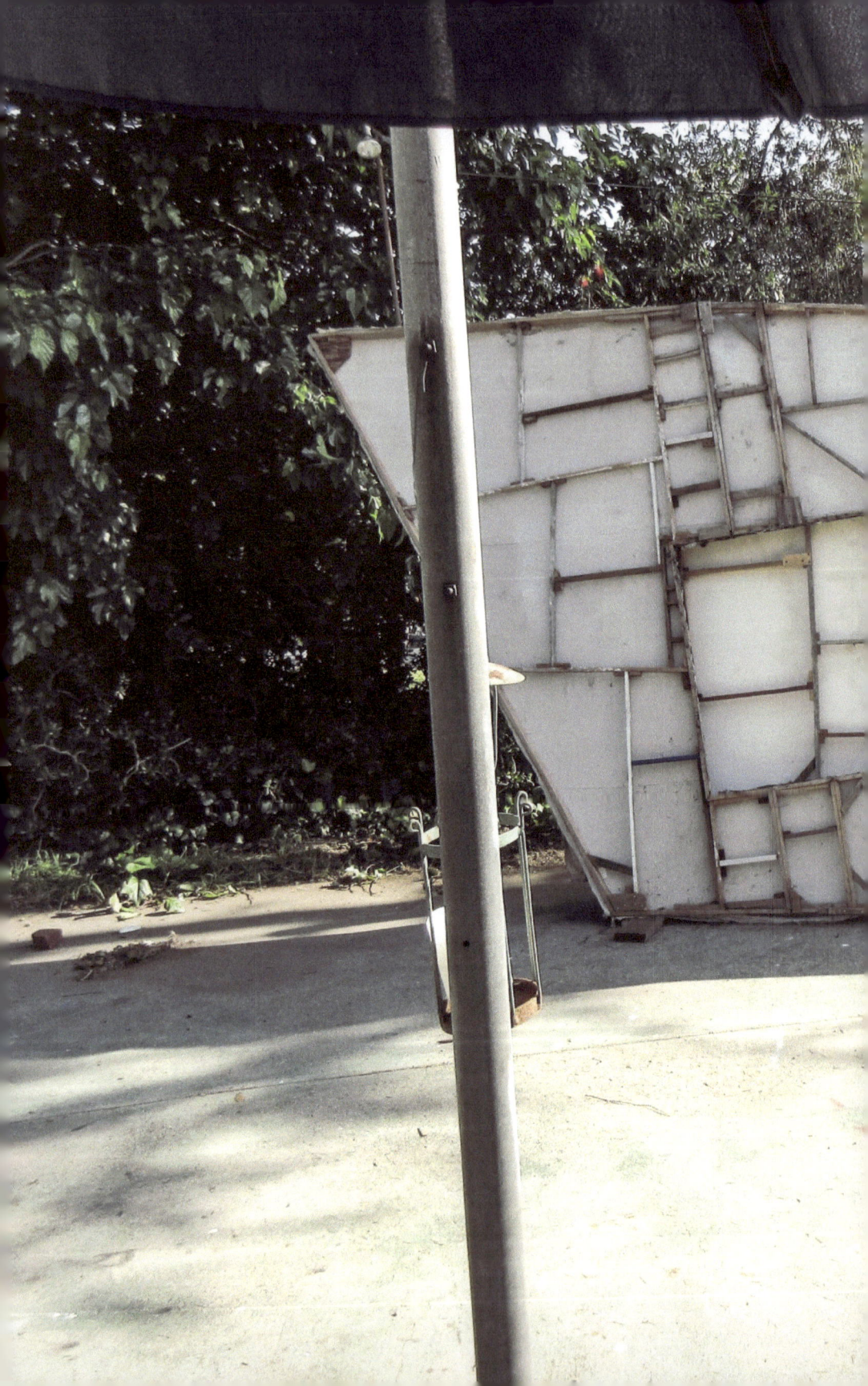

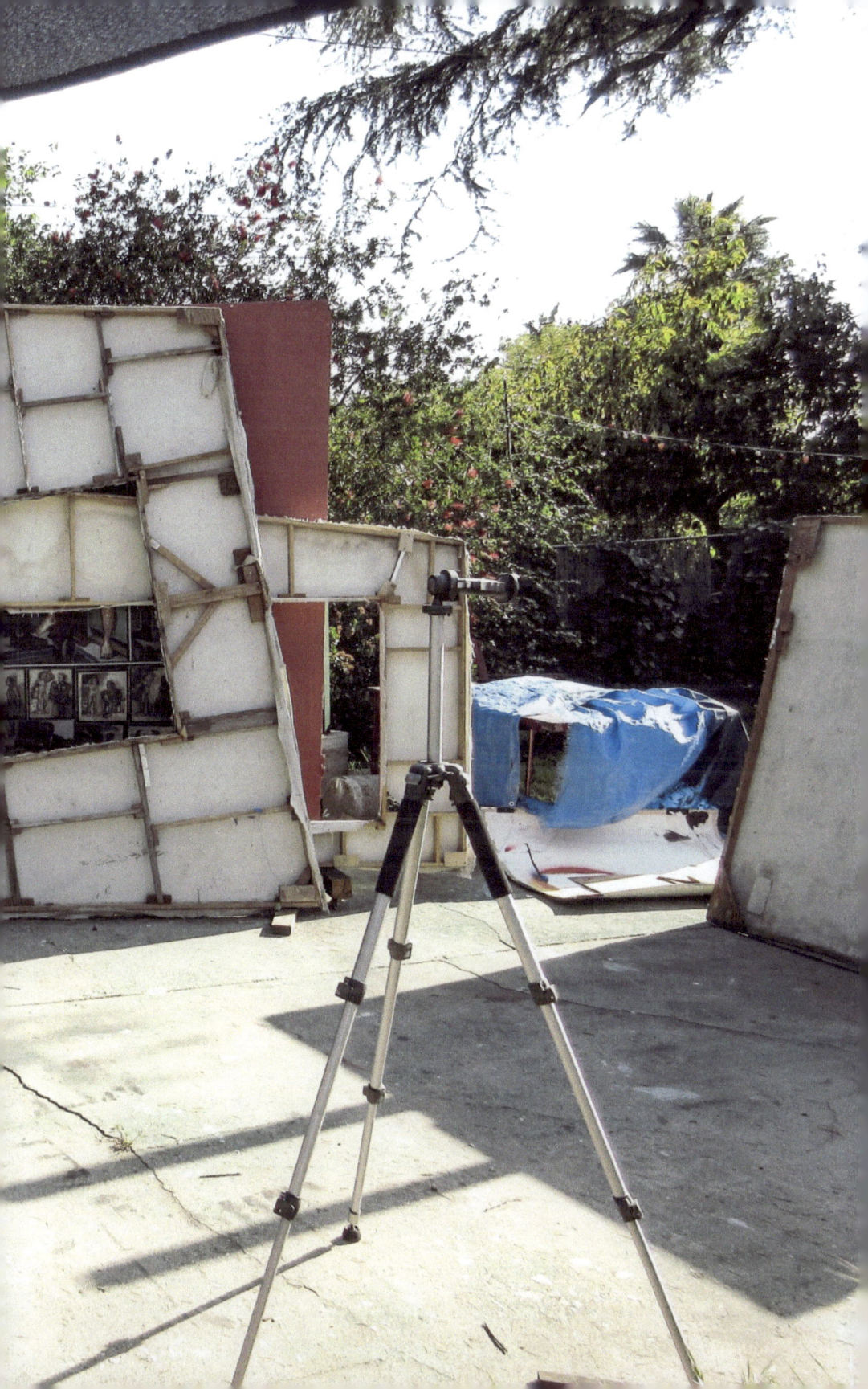

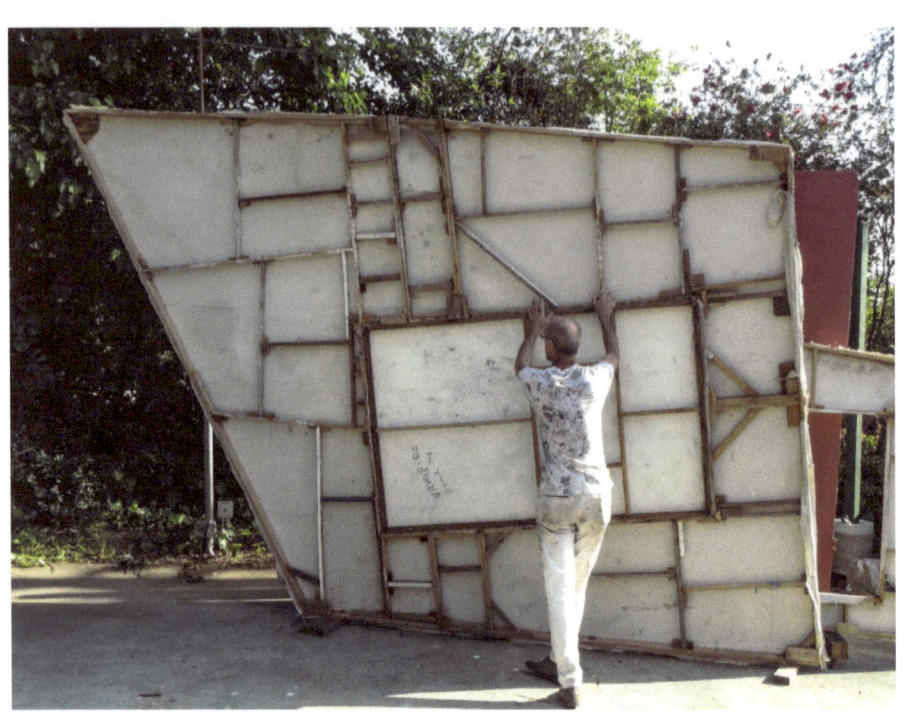
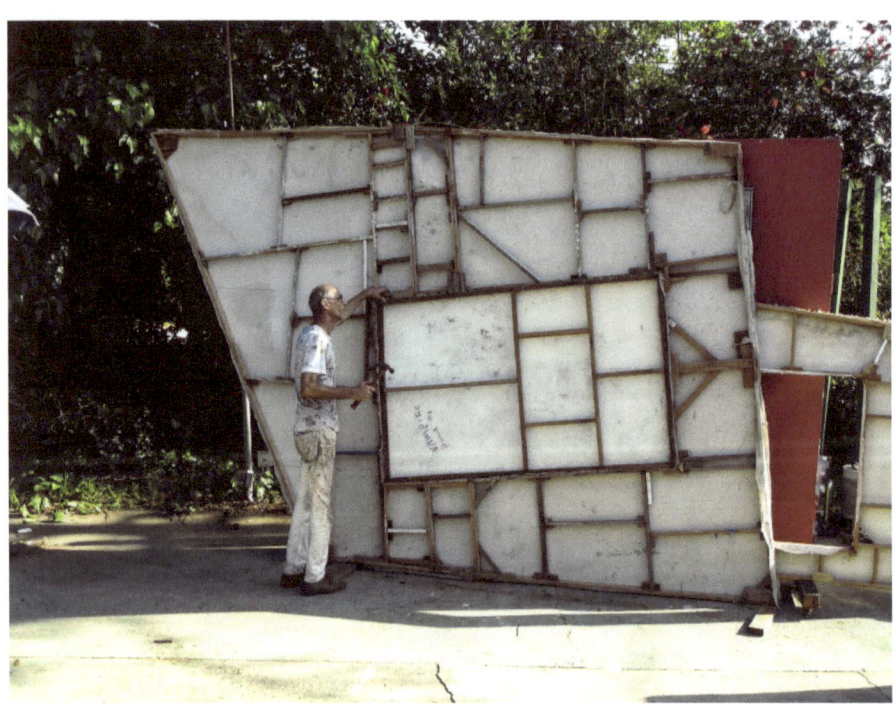

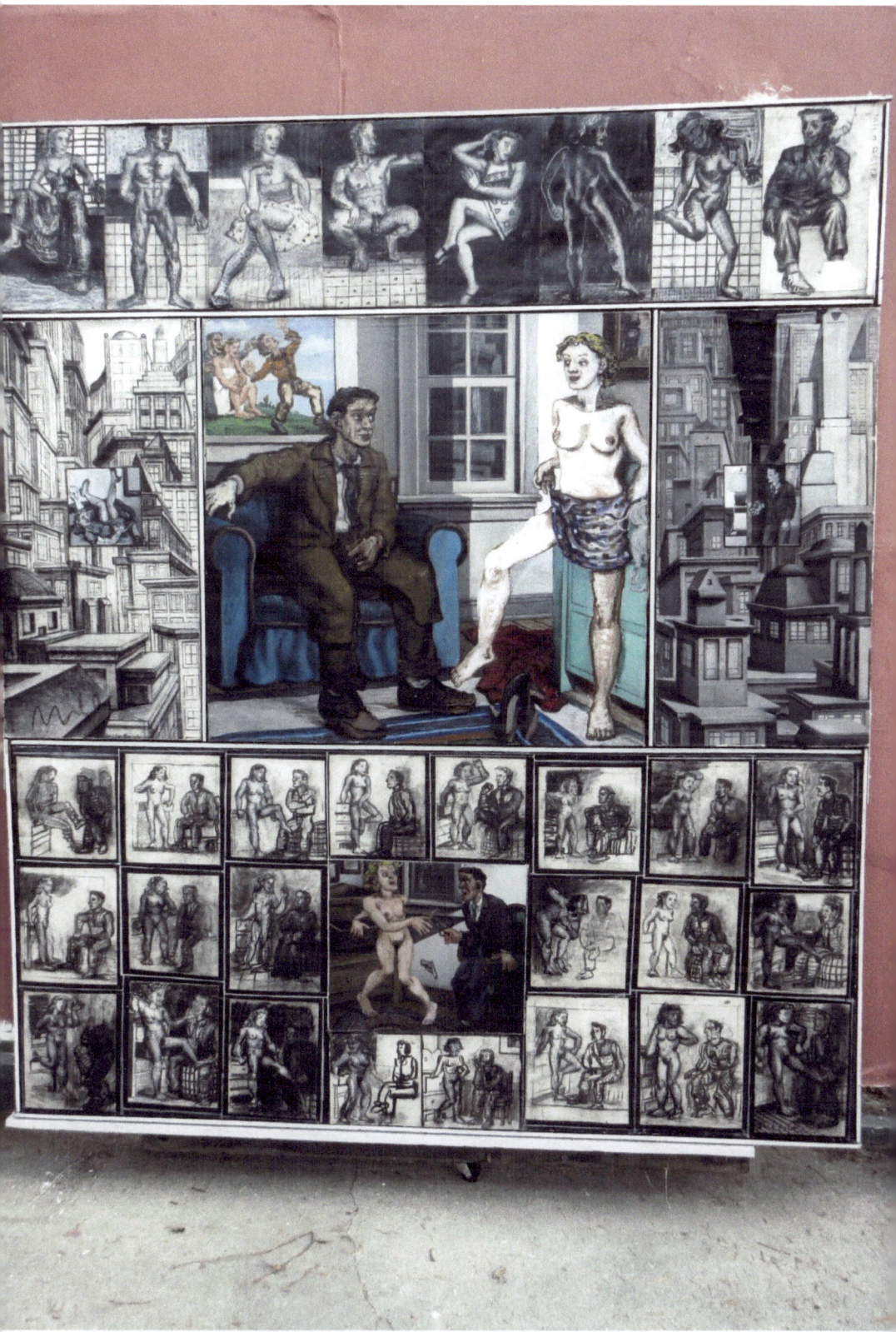

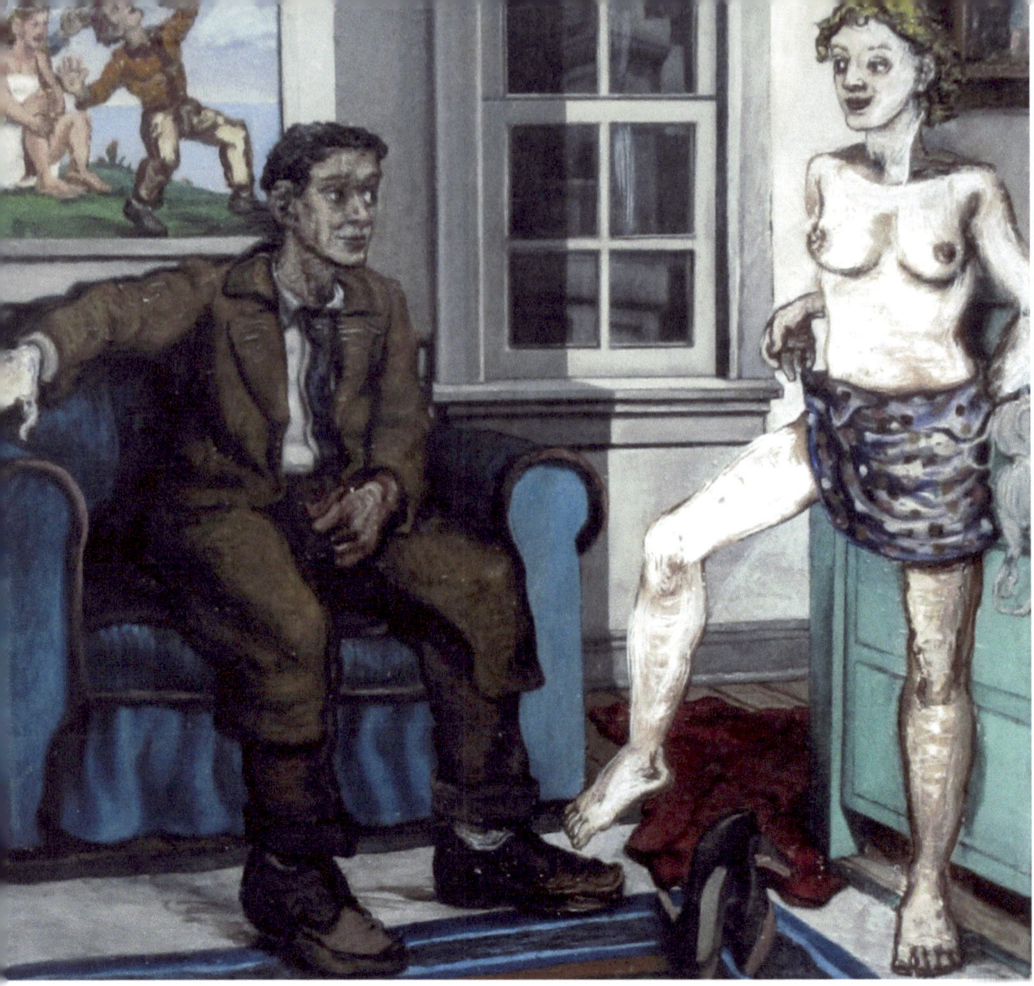

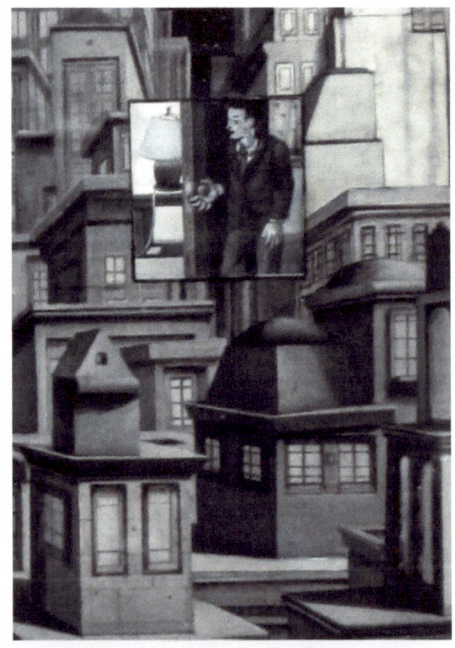

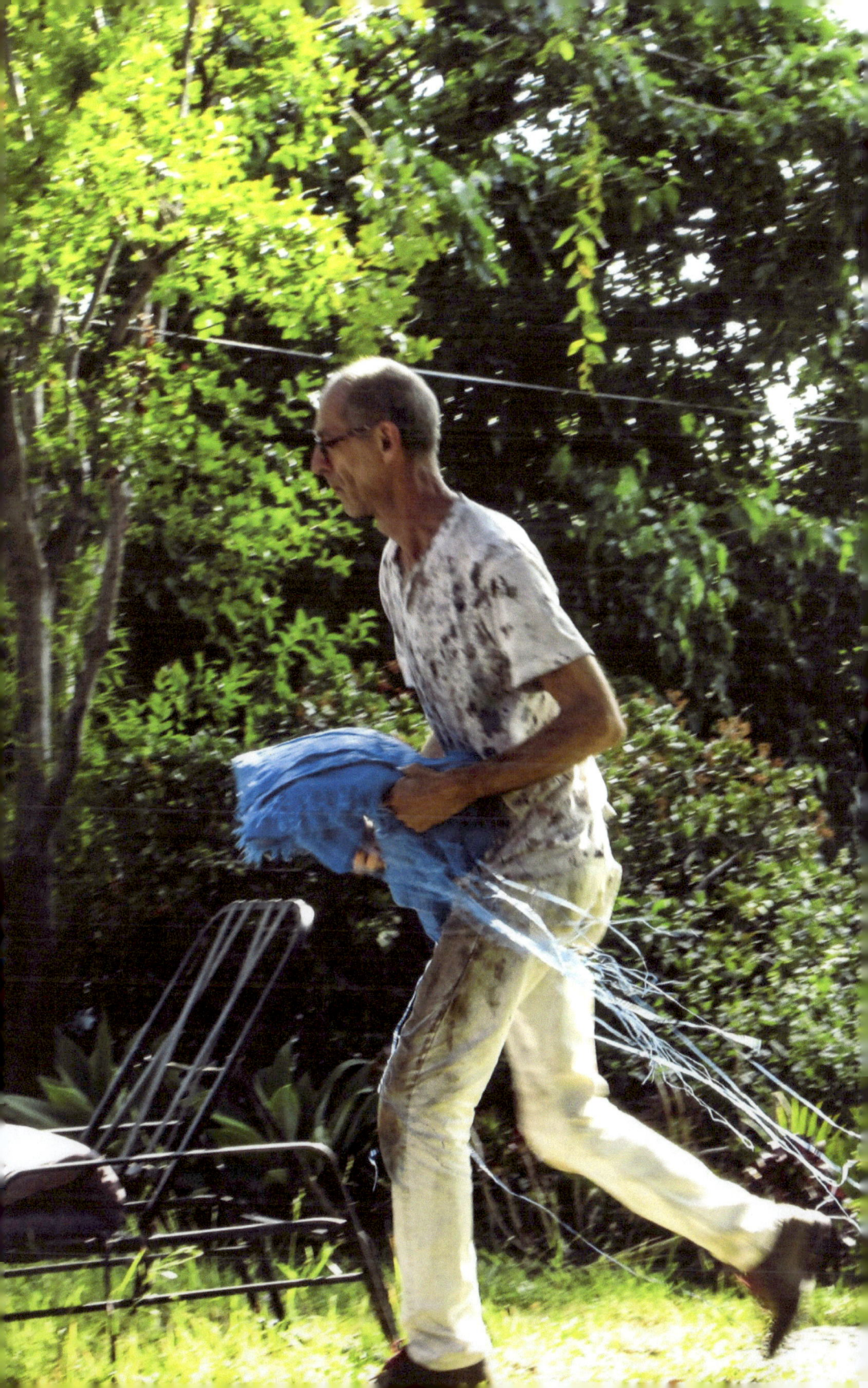

## Enjoy these other books by Paula Sweet

Avanti: *A Love Letter to Ministero del Gusto*
Oasis: *A Love Letter to Rancho Dulce*
Return to Paradise: *A Love Letter to Catalina*

DO NOT – *a book of rules*

*The Grandpa Trio*
Grandpa Goes Shopping
Grandpa Does Yoga
Grandpa Takes A Walk

Paula's Proverbs, Volume I
Paula's Proverbs, Volume II

VSB

The Vicentini

## And these cool titles from 'HcT! Books

111 Haikus

2014 Global Brand Letter
2015 Global Brand Letter

24 Poems by Marco Fazzini

The Blue Tibetan Poppy

The Book of Deals

Case Studies of Five Modern Labyrinths

*The Captain Blackpool Trilogy*
The Crimson Carter
Fate & the Pearls

The History & Adventures of the Bandit Joaquin Murietta

Hitman in Delhi, *a screenplay*

La Toux

Leaving Your Dragon

Legacy & Power

Park Avenue Poop

Supari

Surf City: *A Love Letter to Santa Teresa*

Swami Gopal Buri

Time Out For Dragon!

What Is A Brand?

www.ingramcontent.com/pod-product-compliance
Lightning Source LLC
Chambersburg PA
CBHW041611180526
45159CB00002BC/811